The Art of Universal Success

JOSH RACIOPPO

Copyright © 2022 Josh Racioppo

ISBN: 978-1-922788-08-5
Published by Vivid Publishing
A division of Fontaine Publishing Group
P.O. Box 948, Fremantle
Western Australia 6959
www.vividpublishing.com.au

 A catalogue record for this book is available from the National Library of Australia

All rights reserved. No part of this publication may be reproduced, stored in a retrieval system or transmitted in any form or by any means, electronic, mechanical, photocopying, recording or otherwise, without the prior written permission of the copyright holder.

This book is dedicated to Jim Rohn, who more than a decade ago inspired me to live the best life which I am now living.

INTRODUCTION

The universe is a thing of absolute beauty. It is so abundant that the human mind cannot comprehend its size, its greatness. Then we have this planet we live on. Earth is a masterpiece of art. It is so different from the rest of the universe. As far as we know, earth is a unique place, and it is the only place that we know that can sustain life. But not only can it sustain life, it does so in a magnificent way. Everything we need is here, to let us sustain our lives in every way.

The earth sees to it that we have an abundance of food. It sees to it that we have enough oxygen to live. It provides us with the most splendid things which bring tears to our eyes, like beautiful mountains, magnificent lakes and rivers, and animal life that makes us smile and sometimes makes us laugh. We have everything we need on this planet to live a full life and a life of joy. This is the amazing universe we live in. Everything needed for us to succeed is there in nature.

It is as if everything has been made so that we are able to succeed living on this planet. Things are here to make our lives a rich experience.

If that is the case, then why do we see so many people unhappy and struggling to live? Why are many people unsuccessful in what they do? Why are they not creating a life that is like a beautiful piece of artwork?

One thing I know is that it is not the universe that is at fault. It is not our planet that is the cause of failure. The universe is on our side. The universe wants us to succeed. The sun rises every day to provide life for so many things, including us.

Universal success is all about living a successful life and knowing how we are made and how our planet works and what the universe is made of. Whether we live at the top of the world, at the bottom of the world, in a warm climate or a cold climate, in a country that is thriving or in one that is struggling, we can use universal success and live the life that we want. We can do this because success is what this universe is made to produce.

The planet successfully makes enough food, it provides enough water. It spins at the right speed and stays within the right orbit of the sun. If our planet was a little closer to the sun, we would burn to death. If our planet was a little further from the sun, we would all freeze to death. It is perfect.

The planet earth is a smashing success and because of it the planet's tenants, we human beings, can also be a success if we understand the principles of universal success.

There is an art to living a great life, a successful life. Like an artist studying the very thing he is trying to paint, we can study universal principles as we paint a life of true success and happiness and, when we are done, the canvas of our life will truly be beautiful, like the planet we live on.

I believe in a Creator and that he created the earth to be our home. If you don't believe in a Creator, you can still have faith in universal intelligence and use universal success to live that life that you choose.

I am not a writer. I am an entrepreneur and world traveller. I have dedicated over a decade to studying personal development and trying to understand why one man, living on one side of the road, grows up and is a smashing success at what he pursues and yet another man, living on the other side of the same road, lives a life of struggle, a life of hardship, and is unsuccessful in all that he does. Why is that? Both grew up only metres away from one another.

The reason is that one decided to use universal success principles and the other did not. The one who succeeded may not have even known that he was using universal success principles, but he was and that is why he succeeded.

Success means different things to different people. Success is the ongoing realisation of a worthy ideal. Whatever it is that you want to do and then do, you are a success. It is a journey as well as a destination.

In life, we may come to an intersection where we cannot go straight ahead anymore. We can only go left or right. We can go one way and live by universal success principles and live a happy, satisfying life or we can go the other way, where we live a life of hardship and trouble, not ever being happy with our lives. The choice is up to us. The alternative is to sit at the intersection and just go nowhere.

What is good, is that we have a choice no matter how we were raised, our age, our background, or where we live in the world. We all have a choice and we all can choose a life of happiness and success. If we decide to choose the path of universal success, it will ask us to pay a toll before we proceed down the road. The toll that we will have to pay is discipline, a willingness to work on ourselves. A willingness to put our pride and ego to the side and truly want to be better. On the back of the toll receipt is inscribed what is waiting for us at the end of this road. It is happiness, joy, satisfaction. It says that we can have whatever we want in life. We can live our dreams. We can support ourselves financially and we can help others in need.

If we decide to go the other way, there is no toll for us to pay. The road is wide open. All you will see down this road are warning signs. When we go down this road, it asks nothing of us. It just says that if you continue, then at the end of the road all you will find is unhappiness, struggle, pain, sorrow, victimisation, debt, and a life that has no real satisfaction. A life where one day rolls into the next without any growth.

The interesting thing is that we don't know when we will come to this intersection, when we will have to make a choice. Most people have already reached the intersection and they have chosen poorly.

I write this book in hopes that the reader will make a better choice as they go through this book. A choice of what sort of life they want to live. A life of fun, joy, and happiness, or a life of hardship and struggle. I ask of you to choose the path that will lead you to live the great life that you want to live. Choose that path and choose it today.

Let universal success help you be the best that you can become, and I promise you that if you will change, then everything will change for you and you will be on your way to live the dream life that you want to live. The key to doing this is you.

ONE

In the early parts of World War II, there were many things that Adolf Hitler was not impressed by, including one thing that absolutely infuriated the German leader. A movie was made about him, and the main character of the movie would be an actor imitating him.

That production was called *The Great Dictator*. In the movie, the character that imitated Adolf Hitler was played by Charlie Chaplin. When Hitler saw this, he was upset and banned the movie in the countries he controlled. Chaplin's movie came with a strong message that went against what Hitler stood for.

Charlie Chaplin did a masterful job. I don't know if the depiction was purely to make fun of the German leader or if it was intended to irritate him, but the message did bring into question Hitler's style of leadership.

Chaplin won many awards for his role in the film. His upbringing was a rough one. He was born in a poor district of London, England, on April 16, 1889.

His mother, Hannah Hill Chaplin, was a talented singer, actress, and piano player, but she reportedly spent time in a mental hospital. Charlie's father was a singer, but unfortunately he began drinking and his parents separated. Charlie and his half-brother spent a lot of their childhood in orphanages, where they were often mistreated and beaten if they misbehaved

Charlie was barely able to read and write as a young boy, but he left school and joined a group of comic entertainers. Chaplin starred in the performances this group put on and, by the age of 19, he became one of the most popular music hall performers in England. In 1910 Chaplin went to the United States to perform, became a big star for years, and had a long career in the entertainment industry.

In his life, he had some ups and downs, especially with his morality and political views, but because of the major success all over the world of his acting career, the Queen of England knighted him in 1975. Sir Charles Chaplin died at the age of 88 in 1977.

What Charlie Chaplin showed is that one can have a troubled upbringing, a bad home environment, a past of hurt and pain, and still turn oneself around and live a very successful life. Was it easy for the star to make these changes? I am sure it wasn't, but he did not let the difficulty of it stop him from going after the life that he wanted.

If someone wanted to make the sort of changes that Chaplin had made, he would have to take control of his thinking and would have to reprogram what was taught to him as a child. Charlie was taught one way in the orphanages, but changed that mental programming over the years and made big changes in his life.

When we are born, our mind is completely open to the world. It is open to take in everything and anything that is taught to us. We learn first from our parents. Those little whispers in our ears from our parents as a baby are the beginning of our early childhood learning. Our siblings also have an effect on what goes into our minds, and the family environment plays a massive role in how our thinking is formed as a young person. Then, as the years roll on, we spend time with our relatives, cousins, uncles, and aunties. We see, we hear, we observe. We may not understand everything that is being taught to us, but our mind is taking it all in.

We get a little older and we go to school. At school, we are then taught by our teachers. We start to develop friends at school, and we are constantly learning from them. Throughout this time, our mind is still open and is taking everything in, and we start to be the culmination of all the things we have been programmed with up until then.

As time goes on, we leave school and we get our first job. We now start to learn from our employer and colleagues. We may be in our teens at this point, so our thinking is still developing. Throughout all this time, as we are growing up, we are being influenced by what we watch on TV, the media, and all the people we follow on social media.

All these things and these people are sculpting us into the person we will inevitably become if we allow it and don't try and change what we have been taught. We have now developed a subconscious mind.

Think of two minds, the first a conscious mind and the second a subconscious mind. What we think about, the decisions we make from moment to moment, is coming from our conscious mind. What many don't realise is that all the influences and things we were taught in childhood are now in our subconscious mind.

Let me ask you a question, a personal question just between me and you. How were you raised? Some people were raised well and others had a horrific childhood. If you had a bad childhood, you may not want to think about it, but if you can do so for just a brief moment and no more, think about it and you may realise that your upbringing is the reason why you aren't living the life you want to live.

If you were raised by parents who put you down or who told you constantly that life is hard, life is painful, the universe is out to get you, and that money does not grow on trees, then as an adult these thoughts are stored in your subconscious mind. Then, at the same moment you have a big idea of what you want to do, a little voice that you may not even hear because it is only a whisper says that you can't do it.

Why is that? Is it because your subconscious mind does not want you to have the life that you now want? Yes, that is it. What you want now is going against your very being, the being that for so many years has been one way and which you now want to be another way.

Often, if you start down a path of creating a new life

and a new way of thinking, you may find that you will sabotage your efforts because your subconscious mind thinks in a completely different way, and that's because of those many influential years of growing up.

There are two types of successful people. One is raised by successful parents, parents who taught them that they are valuable and that they can reach any goal that they put their mind to. This person was loved, hugged, and kissed, and their family life was a good one.

Then the other type of a successful person is where the opposite happened. They were raised by people who said they are worthless, maybe they were raised without parents, they may have been homeless, and may have faced many other terrible circumstances. These ones, despite their upbringing, eventually realised the damaging effects of their childhood and reached a point where they had had enough of how they were programmed and made a specific effort to change their life by changing how they think.

The good news is that these two types of successful people can be anyone from any background. Everyone can change how they were programmed, but if we don't make that specific effort then we will go to our default setting, which is the way that we were raised. This is a powerful default setting. It is like when you have a phone. You add many things to the phone, different apps and different settings, and you specifically change how the phone runs. When you sell the phone, you go into the settings of the phone and you do a factory reset. The phone goes back to the way it was when it left the factory. Like that phone, if we don't make a specific hard-fought effort to change, then we are stuck with the default factory settings we were raised with.

That is why earlier I asked you the personal question of how you were raised, because that is your default setting.

Success is available to everyone. You can live the life that you want despite the way you were raised. The hard part is, first, realising that you were raised a certain way and that you may have been programmed for failure and, second, making a specific effort to turn your life around and head in the direction you want to go by reprogramming your subconscious mind.

Despite how you were raised, in the end blaming your parents will do you no good. It is done, nothing can change that. Your parents may have tried their best in raising you but been hindered by how they were raised. World War II was not that long ago. The consequences of that war on how people think have filtered down through the generations. Your parents may have taught you the only way that they know how, because of how their parents taught them. So, blaming will get you nowhere. What will help is the knowledge that you can change all that programming.

Universal success is available to everyone. There are secrets to success and they are secrets not because no one knows about them, but because they are so simple that no one believes them. Universal success is all about knowing how the universe operates. It is knowing how you are made, how your thinking works, and then how applying universal intelligence to your thinking can lead you to a successful life.

I call universal success 'universal intelligence' because it doesn't matter if you believe in God or are an atheist, you can still be successful by knowing how the universe, and you living in the universe, works.

The moment I started to make the changes that led me to the life that I wanted to live was when I realised that I was the reason I was living an unsuccessful life. I realised that if I would change, then everything would change for me, that the problem was not what was on the outside but what was on the inside.

I needed to start reprogramming my mind for success, my thoughts for success. I had to start to change the way I behaved, my attitudes, my discipline, and the most important thing, the things I thought about on a continuous basis.

Many that want to change their life look to things outside of themselves as the cause of why their life is the way it is. People try and change other people to improve their lives, which is like a doctor prescribing medicine to your neighbour that is supposed to help you recover. Many try and change the government in an effort to improve their lives, and this also is not the way to improve their lives. They try and change their boss, their spouse, their friends, and it just doesn't work out for them. The key to success is you. If you will change, then everything will change for you. Start to reprogram your mind for success, not someone else's mind.

As you go through this book, you will see the ways you can go from where you are now to where you want to be. I don't write about specific things, because success is different from one person to the next. What you will see is that, throughout this book, I touch on specific points many times in an effort to make them clear and understandable and memorable.

You can have the life you want by learning about the art of universal success. You can have it if you have what people call a 'paradigm shift'. Your paradigm or pattern of thinking is what has gotten you to where you are today. You are where you are because of the thoughts that you have had up until now. If you want to go further in life and live the life that you want, then you must change how you think.

Albert Einstein said, "We cannot solve our problems with the same thinking we used when we created them."

This is where many people get stuck. They do the same thing over and over again, but expect a different result. You can't think the same thoughts but expect a different outcome. To get different results from what you have now, you need to think differently. You need to change how you think and reprogram your mind for success.

Is it really that easy? Yes, it is. I'm not saying that if we just think happy thoughts then everything that is troubling us will just go away. No, there is still work that you need to do consistently, but your thoughts are where it all begins.

Everyone was raised with a belief system, but that belief system is not necessarily right. This is where it can become difficult, when you have to come to the conclusion that your belief system may be wrong. That is not an easy pill to swallow on the best of days, but it may be necessary to start your journey of change.

Just because our parents taught us their beliefs, that does not necessarily mean that we should adopt them. The unfortunate thing is that we may have adopted them without determining whether those beliefs are good or bad for us.

I often use money as an example because it is easy to quantify. Let's say that your goal is to make one million dollars, but your parents never had any money. They told you as you were growing up that money does not grow on trees, that you have to work hard and long to make a living, and that you should be happy with just scraping by. If your goal is to make a million dollars and you were raised with that belief system, then making a million dollars will be extremely difficult without reprogramming your subconscious mind and changing your belief system. Otherwise, that old belief system will go to work and make sure that you never come close to reaching your goal.

If you were raised by your parents with this belief system, then ask yourself, where did they get this belief system? Did they get it from their parents and their parents get it from their parents and so on? Those beliefs may have been passed on from generation to generation. If your grandparents went through the great depression or either of the World Wars, then their thinking may have been influenced by those events and so they raised your parents with the thinking that life is hard, you have to struggle, and you have to work hard to make ends meet.

Can you see how a belief system can be passed down from generation to generation? Take a moment and think about the belief system you were raised with, and throughout this book I will help you reprogram that belief system into a belief system that will support your goals instead of hindering you from ever reaching them.

This is exciting news because to do the things that you want to do in your life, you don't need to change anything except yourself, and I know that you can do that.

A question that you may be asking is, how do I reprogram my subconscious mind? We will discuss that in the next chapter but, for now, one important thing is this – feel good now. This is something we all can do. We don't acquire happiness, we don't search for it like it is something hard to capture. It is reported that Buddha had been searching for happiness for years when one day he laughed out loud because he realised that we *are* happiness, that happiness is in our DNA and we don't need to search for it. Buddha realised that he had had happiness inside of him all along.

We are born to be happy, it is just part of who we are.

Look at children; they are happy, they may cry for one reason or another, but those little tears go away quickly, because when you remove what is making them unhappy then all that is left is happiness.

Do things that make you happy, but also remove the things that make you unhappy and happiness will be there waiting. This is such an important thing to realise. Once you know this, then you can just appreciate the gift of life. Be grateful for existence, the fact that you have life is an amazing thing.

Having gratitude is so important for a happy, full, and successful life.

This really is the first step of universal success and that is to feel good now.

I know you have it inside of you. Look at a beautiful sunset, look at the stars at night. Maybe it is a beautiful waterfall, or something else, and be happy that you are able to see that beauty.

When you get up in the morning and you start your day, be happy. Hey, you woke up, there were many people who did not wake up this morning, but you did. That should make you feel grateful.

Sometimes we take little things for granted, but if you start your day being happy, then you put your whole state, your whole body, into a good vibration and you will draw other happy people to you.

Many years ago, some monks had to move a big clay statue of Budda in their monastery. While trying to move the statue, a bit of clay broke off and one of the monks saw something shiny underneath. They got their chisels out and started to carve away at the clay statue and what they found underneath the clay was astonishing. The statue was made of gold.

The monks suspected that hundreds of years earlier their forebears had covered the statue with clay for fear of an invading army stealing it. All the monks who knew that a golden Buddha lay underneath the clay were killed and no one knew what the statute was really made of, the value that lay beneath. The gold was always there, it was just covered over.

When you uncover your happiness by removing the things that make you unhappy, then what you will find underneath is like that gold.

Remember that you *are* happiness, you have success and many other good things inside of you. Change your programming and then you will change your life. What awaits you is the life you have always wanted. All that now stands in front of you is one person and that person is you.

Change how you think and you will ultimately change your life and discover the happiness that is inside of you, the happiness that has always been there and is just waiting for you to discover it.

TWO

One day a donkey was walking down a forest path. Thirst and hunger were overwhelming this beast of burden. As the donkey looked ahead to an opening in the road, he noticed from a distance a bale of hay on one side of the opening and a trough of water on the other side. The hay and the water were about twenty metres apart and, as the donkey approached the opening in the road, he found himself in the middle of the two.

What would the donkey do? Would he go to the left and eat some hay or would he go to the right and drink the water? The donkey was frozen with indecision. Not knowing exactly what he wanted and seeing both the hay and water which he needed desperately, the donkey could not move either to the left or the right. Minutes went by and the donkey could not decide, and an hour passed and the donkey was still frozen with indecision. He eventually became weak and lay down. In time the donkey perished because he could not choose between the two things that he needed most to stay alive.

In life, there are many choices to make from moment to moment, choices that can keep us alive or could lead to our death. Then there are decisions to make about what we want to do with our life. Choices that are appealing, that we would be happy with whether we go to the left or the right to get what we want.

But we do need to decide what it is that we want for our lives. If we don't, we will be frozen with indecision and just sit there while life passes us by.

What do you want for your life? This is a question that I ask many people – What do you want? – and it seems to be a hard question for many to answer. Most people kind of know what they want in life, but they have not really spent the time to decide and pinpoint exactly what it is that they want.

I would like to ask you that question again right now – What do you want in your life?

Life is a magnificent gift that we have. Existence, being alive, is something truly precious and many people unfortunately just go through their day trying to get to the next day. Again, I ask – What do you want out of your life? What do you want in the next year, in the next five years or ten years, or what about in the next twenty years?

Do you want to start your own business? Be your own boss and earn as much as you like? Do you have a goal to make one million dollars? Is that your chief aim in life? Maybe it is not necessarily the one million dollars that has all the appeal, so is it the lifestyle that one million dollars can bring you? Could it be that once you reach a million dollars, you might give a lot of it away to charities, to your family, to the needy, to the poor? It may not necessarily be the one million dollars itself that has the appeal for you. It might be the qualities that you will build inside of yourself to reach the one million dollar figure.

Do you want to marry? Do you want to have children? If so, how many? Do you want to buy your first home? Do you want to travel overseas, or maybe travel full-time? Do you want to get out of the city and buy a little cottage on the lake and spend your days feeding the animals? Do you want to be a musician and get paid for doing something that you love? Do you want to be an actor or actress? Do you want to start a charitable organisation and help people in need? Maybe you want lots of money so you can support people with disabilities?

You see, we all want something different for our lives. Success is an interesting word, because it seems to mean different things to different people. Success could be to make one million dollars, be a sports star, play a musical instrument professionally, or paint a beautiful masterpiece that is admired for decades. Chisel a sculpture that would rival the work of Michelangelo or Leonardo Da Vinci, or be an historian who tells tales of old to inspire younger generations.

Success has a wide range of meanings. As I mentioned in the previous chapter, the best definition of success I have come across is that success is the ongoing realisation of a worthy ideal. So, whether it is making one million dollars or playing a musical instrument professionally or getting married and having a family, then as long as you are heading in that direction, you are a smashing success.

Success is the destination and also the journey because if you are on your way to reaching your goal then you are already a success.

But, unfortunately, so many people live an unsuccessful life. They don't know what they want and therefore they never go anywhere. Many people don't live eighty years, they just live one year eighty times.

Success is an art form. It is something that is studied. As an artist creates his art, creating a successful life is also artistic. There is a form to it, a structure that has rich meaning and is something that is learned and put into motion.

Everyone can be successful. We each have that ability. One of the main reasons why many are not successful is, like I said earlier, they don't know what they want. Many have a rough idea of what they want, but many also have no idea.

One way you can find out what it is that you want is to take some time, sit down somewhere quiet, and think about what you really want for your life. What is it that makes you happy, that could get you excited to jump out of the bed in the morning and keep you up late working on in the evening? If you are not sure, then go over all of life's possibilities and see which ones make you smile. That may be a sign of what you want.

You see, if we don't know what we want in life then we are just adrift on the waters of life without our sail up, getting blown about by the wind and the waves, but when we can truly discover what we really want, it is like we have picked a destination and have now put our sails up to go in that direction, no matter what the wind may blow our way.

To tap into universal success, work out what it is that you want, even if it is difficult to do. This is so important in the art of sculpting the life that you want. Know want you want like you know your own name. Let it be that clear for you.

If I ask you, 'What do you want?' and you cannot clearly answer me within three seconds, you are obviously not clear on what you want. You may have a vague idea, but it has no clarity and therefore no effect.

To live a successful life, it must be clear to you, not clear to me or anyone else, just clear to *you*. It may not be easy at the start, but the more you think about it the more clarity you will find.

During the process of discovering what you want, you may realise what it is that you want but think that you will never get it or that you don't deserve it. Don't let those thoughts stop you.

We will talk later about how to overcome those ideas but, for now, just have it clear what it is that you want despite what you may tell yourself. This is the most important step in the art of universal success because if you can't get clear on that, then you will never get what you want out of life and you will live a mediocre life.

I don't want that for you; no one on this planet should

live a mediocre life. I want you to live the best life that you can live. The life where you wake up smiling and happy every day because this way of living is good for you and good for society. You will be the type of person I would like to run into on my journey through life.

Life should be exciting. You exist, you feel, you breathe, you touch, you smile, and life is a wonderful gift.

I hear people say that we all have a purpose in life and we just need to discover that purpose, but I don't believe that we all just have one purpose. Life is meant to be lived in a happy state and we should live whatever life will make us happy, and you don't need to find a purpose. Some people have been looking for their purpose their entire life, and never find it.

Your purpose is whatever you say it is. It is whatever excites you or stimulates you, and living such a life often comes with helping others, being in service to improve the lives of other people.

Why did I say not to worry if you think that you can't have the lifestyle that you want? It is because I know that you can. If another human can do it, then you can do it, as long as it is within the limits of your possibilities. As an example, if a seventy-year-old man who is overweight and out of shape woke up one morning and decided that he was going to run a marathon that day, he would probably not reach the finish line alive.

On that day, that is not possible for him. But making a million dollars, travelling full-time, getting married and having children, moving overseas and learning how to cook in a foreign city, starting your own business, selling up and moving to the lake, becoming a doctor or a lawyer, all these things are possible for you. So, please, don't sell yourself short when you think about exactly what it is that you want in life.

I want you to be successful, but I also want you to be happy, so don't choose a lifestyle that your family wants for you or that your friends want for you. They must walk their own path in life. The thing that you should want is what makes you happy because, whatever you do in life, if you do it unhappily then it is very likely that you will not be a success.

As you study the art of universal success, you can be happy about your decision and then you can go for it at full pace.

Another thing that you should not think about when you are deciding what it is that you want in life, is the how. How you will get the things or the lifestyle you want. This is something that trips up many people on their success journey. They are constantly thinking of how they are going to get it. Not knowing the how is what stops many people from even starting.

You don't need to worry about the how, all you need to do is see as far as you can see, see until the corner in the road, and when you reach that corner then you will be able to see further. Trust that the universe will reveal the how as you go along.

Steve Jobs who founded Apple said that you cannot connect the dots looking forward, it is only when you are looking back that you can connect the dots and see how you got to where you are now.

It is fascinating that the how is what stops so many people. If one day you wanted to drive from one side of the country to the other side, you would not take out the map and mark every single turn that you would need to take to reach the other side. All you would do is mark where you are starting and then start heading in that direction until you need to turn and then you would get your map out again and see where it is that you need to turn next. You know that, as long as you are heading in that direction, you will reach your destination.

So don't think about the how, how you will get to the life you want, because the how may not even be on your radar. You can only see a certain amount of the picture, and there are so many things that are off your radar that you cannot yet see how you will get to where you want to go.

In the late 1800s, two brothers who owned a bicycle shop had a dream to fly. They had one goal and it was not just to see a manned glider soar through the air, because others had done that. Their vision was of a pilot being in a position to mechanically fly a winged aircraft. Others had tried to steer gliders, but unfortunately one particular person who had a big impact on the brothers died in a gliding accident. The brothers knew that it was possible to mechanically steer an aircraft as it continued flying. Engines had already been invented, wings were around, but the Wright brothers had a vision of control by the pilot on board and one day in 1903, at Kitty Hawk, the first controlled powered flight took off and made history.

These men had a goal, a vision, and despite the risk of death before them, they were relentless. If they had not been clear on exactly what they wanted, then when the challenges and fear came, they would have given up. At the start they didn't necessarily know how they were going to do it because it took a while to work it all out, they just knew they would.

So don't worry about the how. If you follow the steps that are laid out in this book, the how will come to you. Amazing things and events will align to get you to where you want to go.

Please spend the time to search inside of yourself for what it is exactly that you want. Once you know what it is, write it down in a short sentence and in the positive. Write it as if you are already there, as if you are living that life right now.

As an example, you might write, *I am so happy and grateful now that I am…* and finish the sentence. Laminate this little card that has the specific thing that want and carry it with you wherever you go. You should take the card out a few times a day and read your statement out loud and feel the feelings of having the life that you want. This may sound silly to some, but what this does I will explain in another chapter because I mention this process a few times in this book. For now, though, just doing this will put you in a good and happy frame of mind.

If the card is in your pocket, then throughout the day, when you put your hand in your pocket, it will bring to mind the life that you are heading towards, and the good feelings from that will do wonders for you.

As I said, we will discuss how your thoughts work more soon, but another thing I recommend that you do is start to be the person you want to be in the future, start to act like that person would act and talk, and present yourself like someone who already has the life you want.

If you want to be a millionaire, then start to act like a millionaire, think like a millionaire, talk like a millionaire, shake hands like a millionaire. Watch millionaires and see how they act.

If you want to be in a loving relationship, then think of the good qualities that you want in your partner and start to be that person today, the person who shows those qualities in their day-to-day life. If you want someone who is loving, then start to be loving. If you want someone who is fair, then be fair; if you want someone who is genuine, then please be genuine.

If you want to travel more, then act like a traveller, buy travel gear, go to travel shows, have travel maps around your home, act and be like a traveller. Study the history of the countries that you want to visit.

Whatever it is that you want in your life, act now as if you are already there, already be that person today as you head in that direction. If you can hold it in your mind, then you can hold it in your hand.

A very important step in getting you to where you

want to go is visualisation, where you spend a few minutes in the morning and the evening visualising what it is that you want. Not only visualising what you want but also feeling the feelings of already having it. I would suggest that you find a quiet place in the morning and evening and, with your eyes open or closed, visualise the life you want.

Your goal may be to earn a certain amount of money every month. If that is the case, you can visualise yourself going to your bank with a cheque, with your name on it and with that amount written on it, and depositing it in the bank. Hear the sounds all around you as if you were there. Visualise your bank statement with the amount that you want coming in every month. Why not photo-edit one of your bank statements now and then put in the amount, month after month, that you want to earn and put that in a place where you can see it regularly.

Think and feel what it will be like to spend the money that you will earn, the places you want to go to, the clothes you would buy, the fancy restaurants you would like to frequent.

What about if you want to be in a loving relationship? In your visualisation time, visualise being with someone, don't choose a specific face, just someone that you are having dinner with, someone whose hands you are holding. Picture yourself walking down a romantic street somewhere, visualise yourself in the park having a picnic. Visualise anything that can make you feel now as if you are in that relationship. Why not go the extra mile;

if you have a two-car driveway, why not park your car on one side of the driveway and leave an empty spot for your future partner?

Clear room in your closet for the clothes that your future partner will have. Eat at the table and make another place setting for this person. Throughout the day, visualise yourself already having what you want. When you eat breakfast, think about it. When you are having a shower, think about it. When you are driving your car, think about it. Whenever you can, visualise already living the life that you want. Feel the feelings of it being here now.

This works with anything that you want. I am just using the example of money and a romantic relationship because they are easy to visualise, but it works with all things.

Whatever you think about on a regular basis is what you will get.

One thing that you can do that is also important is exercise gratitude. Being grateful for what you have already is what will help you get what you want.

If you are not grateful for things now, then there is a chance that you won't reach your destination. If you are upset and unhappy when you try to go after what you want in life, that journey will be a hard one. Why not make it easier by putting your mind in a good state regularly?

Every morning, take a few minutes and go over in your mind all the things that make you feel grateful, the things that make you feel appreciation.

Don't only think about these things, but also feel feelings of gratitude. Make the feelings well up inside of you.

Be grateful for your family, for your life. Existence is a tremendous gift, the fact that you can live and feel joy and love. Feel those feelings of gratitude.

When you start your day with this, and not with terrible news, you will put your whole body into a great vibration.

Do this daily please and with this alone you will see great results. We will touch on these techniques a few times in this book.

I don't personally know you, but I feel that you are my friend and I call you my friend because you are on this journey that I am continually on and have been on for over a decade, a journey of self-improvement and joy. We are kindred spirits. We are all connected, this universe is an amazing creation and it is on our side. Most successful people think so. The unsuccessful think that the universe is against them. It's me against the world, they say.

It does not need to be that way. Believe me when I say that the universe is on your side.

We will soon discuss how that is in more depth, but if you wake up and expect good things to happen to you, then they will. It is not luck, it is your thinking that attracts things into your life via the person that you become. I have seen so many negative people continually receiving negative results in their life, and I see positive people constantly attract positive things into their lives.

This is not luck, it is attraction. You become what you think about.

The universe wants to do you good. When I say the universe, I mean the entire universe of Creation. It is geared to respond to how you think.

In my previous book *Think and Be Unstoppable*, I talked about how our thoughts create our world and in this book I will go a little deeper, but I will keep it simple so you can start to practise universal success thinking and completely transform your life.

Unfortunately, there are people out there who are truly nasty. You may run into one of these people from time to time, because they move around a lot, but every now and again the storm does come into your life. It is in those moments that universal success thinking will help you. It will help you when you have strong enough reasons to succeed.

You see, reasons are what will pull you through when the storm comes, the reasons why you want what you want.

Let's take money as an example. Let's say that you want to make one million dollars. Why do you want to make one million dollars? Is it to help the poor, support your family, give to a charity, start a not-for-profit organisation? You see, those reasons will be the strength that holds you to the ground, so you don't get swept up and away by the storm.

Once you have what you want clearly in mind, get enough reasons for it, and write what you want on a card to carry with you, then you will start heading in the direction you want to go with your life.

There are many things that we have briefly spoken about that you should do if you want to change your life and start heading in the direction of your ideal life. This is where we come to an intersection on the left or right. Many won't take these steps for multiple reasons, some because they say they don't have enough time, which is never true. Others because they think that they can reach their goal without doing them, but the truth is that people who truly succeed in life, live a disciplined life and have daily success habits that make them successful. Don't let this book just be a feel-good book.

One day I was speaking with a bank manager who was setting up the accounts for one of my businesses. We spoke about personal development and he told me that he attended a seminar years ago that was given by a famous person in the personal development field. He said he felt great for a week after, but he stopped doing the things that he learned and not much changed in his life. He said that he thinks he should pull out his notes from that weekend one day and go over them, but I don't think he ever will.

You see, the biggest mistake people make is not taking the action that is needed on a consistent basis.

So please, do take the actions mentioned in this book. Do them regularly and not only will you start to feel great on a regular basis, but you will start to see results fairly soon and these early results are what will keep you going.

I have great faith that you are a person who is serious, and only the serious will succeed. Put all doubt aside and start today and you will see your life start to change, and then one day you will look back at who you were and you won't even recognise the person that started this journey because you will have completely changed and you will start to live the dream life that you have always wanted to live.

THREE

One day a man was walking in the desert. The sun was beating down on him and he was thirsty, exhausted, and lost. He had no idea where he was, and the sun was not going down anytime soon. After some time of not knowing where he was, the man noticed a small hut in the distance. When he arrived, he couldn't believe his eyes; there in the middle of the hut was a water pump that could be operated by hand. He started pumping and pumping, but to no avail; not even a drop of water came. He was getting tired and frustrated. He thought to himself that there must be no more water left.

Suddenly, he noticed a big bottle of water in the corner of the room. He was relieved that he had finally found water. As he approached the water bottle, he noticed a little piece of paper on the top of the bottle that had a message on it saying, *This water is to be used to prime the water pump. Please don't forget to fill this bottle up before you leave, so the next person can use the pump.*

What should the man do? The water looked clean, so he could drink it straight out of the bottle, but then he would have no more than just that one bottle of water.

The other option was, he could just trust the person who wrote the message and use that water to prime the pump. In doing this, the risk was that, if the pump still did not work, he would have no water whatsoever.

What should he do?

The man hesitantly and carefully poured all the water in the bottle into the pump and started pumping. After a few seconds of pumping, he heard some gushing sounds and then the water started to pour out. The man was saved, he was going to live.

After drinking all the water he needed, he looked around the room and found a map of the area. He now discovered where he was and was now able to find his way out of the dessert. While looking around the room, he found a pencil that was with the map. He refilled the water bottle for the next person and he pencilled in under the original message the words, *Please trust me, it really works*. The man then left and started heading towards his destination.

This man thought that water was scarce in the area because he was in a desert. In his mind he had no idea that there could be any water in a desert. The fact is that the water was abundant, it was everywhere, he just could not see it.

The universe is an abundant place, ever-expanding. Look around and see all the abundance that surrounds you, nothing is scarce. Think of all the water in the oceans, in the rivers, flowing down from the sky. Think of the mountains and the waterfalls that are so beautiful.

Think of all the water that flows through the pipes in your city and in your home. Think of all the trees that are everywhere. What about all the leaves on all the trees and each blade of grass. The stars in the heavens are abundant and make the night sky come alive.

Think of people, they are everywhere you look. Food is abundant. Even in developing countries there is usually an abundance of food. What about emotions like love? Love is abundant, like the love in families, the love between couples and close friends. Have a stroll down a boardwalk in the evening and see the loving couples walking along together hand in hand.

What about money? There are massive amounts of money everywhere in the world, in both poor countries and rich countries. Go visit cities on the French Riviera like Monte Carlo in Monaco. You will see money in abundance.

What about in your city? Think of all the money in the shops, the buildings, people's wallets. Money is everywhere.

Take time and think about this deeply, about just how abundant life and everything in life is, because the one thing that holds many people back from achieving their goals is that they think that what they want is scarce, hard to come by, but that is not the case.

If you want to be in a loving relationship, love is everywhere. If you want to have more money, it is everywhere in abundance. If you want a happy life, happiness is in abundance. If you want to start your own business, there are successful businesses everywhere you look. Take time and think about this and know that abundance is everywhere.

Your thoughts may be stopping you from having what you want, because you may have developed a scarcity mentality. The scarcity mentality often comes from a belief that you were raised with. I spoke about this earlier, that many people were raised with the scarcity mentality, the thinking that money doesn't grow on trees.

There are people I know for whom money does grow on trees in many ways. Money flows in and out of their lives like a summer breeze. One of the reasons for this is that they do not have the scarcity mentality.

One thing that many people who want to have more money do is hold onto the money that they have because they think that if they don't hold onto it tightly, it will run away and won't come back.

From now on, start to think differently. Take on a new pattern of thinking and believe that money flows in and out of your life. There is a universal law that if you want to receive something, then you need to first give it. This is hard for many people to believe. The important thing with this law is that you don't give just to receive, you give because it helps others and in turn it brings you joy, and the universal outcome is that you will get it back and get it back in greater abundance.

I assume that you already know about this universal law, because I'm sure that you know it works with other things. If someone came up to you and asked how they could have more love in their life, would you not tell them to first give love? If you want kindness, what do you do? You give kindness first. If you want a smile, start smiling first.

So, if these things work in all these other areas, then wouldn't it be the same with money? If you want more money, then give money and give not to receive but because it will bring you joy to give to those who need it. I am not saying to give away everything you have tomorrow, but start regularly giving an amount you are able to give.

What this does is change how you think and then that thinking will affect your subconscious mind. Thinking that money is easy to come by and that you will always have plenty of it affects your subconscious mind and it starts to believe that this is so. Then your whole body is in the right energetic state to start attracting things, people, and situations into your life which will open doors for you to get more money. Yes, when those doors open up, you will have to take massive action. Opportunities will present themselves when you are regularly in that state, but you will need to take action.

If you continue to have a scarcity mentality, then money will stay away from you. If you don't first give love, then love will stay away from you. Many businesses do fail these days, and not because there is not a market for what they are offering. There is a market for everything these days. They fail because they are so scared that they will not succeed, and then of course they don't.

Like Henry Ford said, "If you think that you can or think that you cannot, you are right." Your thoughts, your scarcity mentality, are what will stop the very thing that you want to come into your life, whether it be money, love, joy, or anything that you want.

What are some practical steps for you to take to overcome a scarcity mentality? It is simple, but not easy. Like I said earlier, you must change your belief system. I am sure that if your goal is to make more money, you won't just empty your bank account and give it all to the poor. Giving to the poor is great, but this is not the way to go about it. If you give, make sure it is because you want to give and not just because you want to receive in turn.

I would suggest starting small. If there is something that you intended to sell, don't sell it but give it away with joy, because there is more happiness in giving than there is receiving. I am not saying give away your house or your car rather than selling them, but if you have a phone that you were going to sell, give it away. If you were going to have a garage sale, don't sell the items, give them away. A fridge, a TV, anything like that, don't sell it, give it away for free and do it with all your heart. This will start changing how you think about money.

Another thing that you can do that will help you to eliminate a scarcity mentality is something that I wrote about in my first book, and that is to go to the bank and get thirty one-dollar coins or notes and each day for a month leave a dollar somewhere where someone will find it. Don't give it away, just leave it somewhere. After thirty days, if you can afford it without starving, then get thirty two-dollar coins and do the same. Then again in thirty days if maybe you are reluctant to leave this small amount of money, then up it to thirty five-dollar notes and do the same thing; leave a five-dollar note somewhere each day for thirty days where someone will find it. You can vary these amounts depending on your income and which country you live in, but by doing this you will discover the level of scarcity mentality you have regarding money.

If after thirty days you still struggle to leave that one-dollar coin somewhere every day, then just keep doing that until it is easy to do before you move on to the bigger amounts. Play around with this, view it as a game and have fun with this, because you will come to realise in time that it will be easier and easier for you to give away money. After all, money flows in and out of your life.

No one likes a rich person who is like Ebenezer Scrooge and wants to accumulate all the money he possibly can get and hold onto it tightly because he is just so in love with having money.

Many wealthy people in fact love giving, because it brings them joy and they know they will always have an abundance because they do not have a scarcity mentality.

There was a rich man once who had so much money that, before he died, he wanted to give it all away. So, he started giving it away to people who he thought were worthy of it and would use it for worthy causes. When he died, he had about ten times as much money as when he first started to give it away. Money goes to where it is welcome, not to where it will be locked in a room never to be spent. This applies to anything that you want in life, not just money.

There is a reason why roughly three percent of the population have about ninety-five percent of all the money. Yes, they do have good businesses and, yes, they may have inherited a lot of it from their families, but the reason why they continue to have it is because they don't hold onto it so tight that they can't let any of it go.

You will find that a lot of greedy people are people who have little money. They are so desperate to get it all for themselves. You will find that the ones whose thinking is consumed by holding onto money and securing it, and who are scared that they will lose it, are the ones who end up losing it all because they become what they are thinking about.

I was speaking with someone recently who often says that he cannot afford this or cannot afford that. I instructed him to change his thinking. When you tell yourself that you cannot afford this or afford that, then you will never be able to afford it. You are telling your subconscious mind that you can't afford it, and that is the exact situation you will keep attracting into your life.

Start a process to begin to eliminate this sort of 'I can't afford it' mentality. Even if your goal is only to increase your income just a little, begin the process so as to change how you think about money. Money is not evil, only the love of it is. I think you are a person who is not in love with money.

Next time you want something, ask yourself, what can I do to afford it? That is a much better question because what it does is open up your thinking to finding ways to afford it and attracting things into your life which will enable you to afford it.

Your thinking controls your world and to change your thinking may take a little time, especially if you were raised with a scarcity mentality. I talk about money a lot because this is where most people want to improve their lives, but your goal is your goal. Like I keep saying, I don't promote wealth and I don't promote poverty, it's your life and your decision. But I assume there are a lot of people who do want to increase their income, maybe even double it, so removing this scarcity mentality is important.

Your goal may be that you want to travel more. If that is the case you will need a little more money, so don't tell yourself that you have no money to travel. Rather, ask yourself the question, what can I do to travel more? If you want romance, don't tell yourself that you don't deserve romance, tell yourself that you deserve romance and ask yourself, how can I get more romance in my life? What do I need to do starting today to attract romance?

If you want to play a musical instrument, don't tell yourself that you have no talent because if you do that, you won't even start. Rather, ask yourself, how can I learn a specific musical instrument? How can I develop talent to play this instrument? What about if you wanted to play that instrument professionally? Don't say that there are not many jobs out there for musicians. No, that would be scarcity thinking. You have to change that thinking to thinking that there is an abundance of jobs out there which you could get playing this instrument.

What about if you wanted to become an actor or actress? Many who start off pursuing these careers don't end up reaching their goal because in their minds they are telling themselves that there aren't enough acting jobs out there for them and it is so hard to get a job in the entertainment industry and, with that sort of thinking, that is exactly what they get, no job. They should be telling themselves that there is an abundance of acting jobs out there and that they will reach their goal. They should then ask themselves, what can I do to improve my skills in this area?

These are just a few examples of a scarcity mentality and how we can start changing the way we think. Changing your paradigm about abundance won't happen in twenty-four hours, but it will happen if you continue to watch what you think about and watch the type of words you speak, either silently or out loud, because words have power.

Money is abundant, love is abundant, travellers are abundant, music is abundant. This universe is all about abundance. Start to change your thinking and come to the same conclusion. Every morning, get up and look out your window and notice the things that are abundant. As you go about your day, notice the abundance everywhere, the buildings, the trees, the cars, the people. Those things are everywhere and that is the same with the very thing that you want in your life. The universe is abundant and it is on your side. It is time for you to truly believe this and live the life that you have always wanted to live.

FOUR

One day I decided to buy a new car. I was sitting in the showroom and having a nice discussion with the salesman. We were talking about personal development and self-improvement. He told me about his sales past and how nearly ten years ago he was mentoring a young man who was starting in the industry. He wanted to help him improve in the field of sales. This salesman obviously had many years of sales experience himself.

After our discussion, I bought the car and left. One week later, I returned to take delivery of the vehicle and the salesman greeted me excitedly. He said that he had something to tell me. We sat down and he began telling me that, in the week since we talked, he had received an email from someone he had not spoken to in many years. The person that emailed him was the very young man that he had mentioned to me the week before. Having not been in contact for years, the young man he trained emailed the salesman and said how thankful he was and how he appreciated all the advice and training that he had received. The salesman said to me, "Can you believe it? We were just talking about this young man and, after all these many years, I get an email from him?" This salesman was very surprised, but I was not. It fitted in perfectly with how I know the universe works.

Have you ever had something similar happen to you? Maybe you were thinking about someone and all of a sudden you got a phone call from them? Some just call it a coincidence but, in my experience, it happens too often for it to be just coincidence. I believe that there are some coincidences in life, but when you know how the universe works and what it is made of, then you know how to get what you want.

In this section, I will talk about universal laws and principles. I am going to let you decide what you believe once you see how the universe works, and then you can use that knowledge to create the life you want. I will tell you about the science behind it, but I want you to come to whatever conclusion you like.

People talk about the 'law of attraction'. You may have heard the term. They say it means there is a connection between the thoughts you have and what you attract into your life. Some don't believe it, and some do. I want you to decide for yourself. To know if the law of attraction works, you need to know how the universe works and then it is up to you whether you believe it.

They say the law of attraction is not just that you become what you think about. Experts say it goes deeper than that and it is you attracting what you yourself are. How could this attraction work?

What is everything made up of? What are you made

up of? What is the table you see made up of? What is the pencil on your desk made up of? What is the coffee cup made up of? If you listened to your science teacher at school, you would know that it is atoms. There are different kinds of atoms, but we will try and keep this simple. When you look deeper within the atom, you see the nucleus of the atom. The nucleus is made up of protons and neutrons together. Revolving around this nucleus are the electrons, constantly in motion. I won't go into electrons acting either like a wave or a particle. As I said, I will keep this simple.

The electron is moving around the nucleus of protons and neutrons, and all of this vibrates, has a frequency. Think of it as energy, like electricity. How it all moves, and its type of vibration, is what determines what it is. All things are made of these atoms and their nuclei and the moving electrons.

To simplify it, the thing that makes a table a table, a pencil a pencil, is just the vibration of what is below the atom, its electrons, protons, and neutrons, its frequency. Whether it is rocks on the moon or dirt in the garden, it is made of the same atoms, it just has different vibrations, the electrons move differently.

Knowing this is important because once you know it, then you know what your body is made up of. It is all atoms.

An interesting thing that scientists have found is that your thoughts have substance, and consciousness has an effect on matter. If your thoughts affect matter, then you can realise that thoughts can become things.

Albert Einstein said, "Everything is energy and that is all there is to it. Match the frequency of the reality that you want, and you cannot help but get that reality. It can be no other way, this is not philosophy, this is physics."

We are all connected, everything is energy. It is the building block of the universe. Scientist have known for over a hundred years that everything vibrates and that everything is energy. So, whatever it is that you want, it is energy. Like Einstein said, you need to match the energy of the thing that you want. It is like magnets but without limits on distance. It is amazing how much energy is everywhere. The planet itself has a magnetic force that even birds pick up and act upon.

This is the science about how the universe works, in simple terms. Have you ever noticed that negative people tend to attract negative things into their lives? Do you also notice that positive people tend to attract positive things into their lives? Things just seem to work out for them. Some say that this is luck. But it's not luck, these ones have a pattern of thinking positively, so they match the frequency of positive things and then get them.

I personally believe that our thoughts have substance. We think of all the bad things that could happen and we start to stress. That stress then affects our health. If thoughts had no substance, I don't think stress would exist, because how could something that has no substance affect something like your body, which is substance? Thoughts are powerful, they can affect your health and even end your life prematurely if stress is not reduced. Have you come across someone and felt negative vibes that they are throwing off? I am sure you have. You can just sense it, can't you?

The 'law of attraction' is called that because people say it works like a law, that it happens every time like gravity, that it is consistent. You become what you think about.

One person described the law of attraction as having a dominating idea, a plan, a purpose. This idea is then held in the mind of a person. It is there through repetition of thought. If this idea is held in the mind with strong emotions and a burning desire for its realisation, then this burning desire affects the subconscious mind and then it is acted upon through whatever natural or logical means are available.

I do believe that if you have a burning desire for what you want, then that will affect the subconscious mind. If there is no burning desire, then there is no effect. The burning desire is like the fuel that makes a rocket launch. A key point is that, whatever the desire is, you must want it with all your heart.

If there is hesitancy or you just want it, but without burning desire, then you won't attract it into your life.

You don't get what you want, you get who you are. What you want has to be you. You have to be the person that you want to be before you can become that person.

If this is true and thoughts become things, then what have you been regularly thinking about? Your thinking has gotten you to where you are now and, if you want to go further, the thoughts that you have had up to now will not be enough. You need a different thought pattern to get you from where you are now to where you want to be.

This is a very brief and simple description of how the universe works. Some people believe that the law of attraction works even if you don't do anything except use your thoughts to attract everything that you want. Others believe that that doesn't work, that you must take massive action and that is what will make you a success, without much thought or burning desire. Some say that using the law of attraction just increases the chances of getting what you want. Yet others believe that you become what you think about and if you have a burning desire for that thing, you will take appropriate action and will get it, as long as the thing that you want is in abundance.

As you go through this book, I want you to come up with how you think the universe works. I do believe that thoughts become things and you become the person that you think about on a regular basis.

What can you start doing straight away to start attracting good things into your life? The first thing is to feel good now. This is something that most people don't try to do. They may naturally feel good now, but many people just go through the day feeling the emotions that the day brings.

When you take an active role in making sure you focus on how you feel, then when you are not feeling the best, you won't just continue in that state. You will change the way you are feeling and the way you are thinking. Focus on doing the things that make you feel good now. This is different for everyone. Work out some things that you can do now to get you from feeling bad to feeling good, because if you stay in the state of not feeling good, then you will just attract things into your life that don't make you feel good because your thoughts are not focused on feeling good.

You might say to me that it is not always easy to feel good now, and I completely understand that. You may have all sorts of things going wrong in your life because of what you have been thinking about up to now. If you can't start focusing on positive things, things that normally make you smile, things that make you feel good, then what you may need to do is to have a 'state change'.

Often when you are not feeling good, your body is moving in a certain way because it is following how you are thinking. At this point it may be necessary to have a physical state change. If you are not feeling good, you may need to start moving your body. You may need to get up and stretch. Maybe put on your running shoes and get some exercise. Maybe get your towel and go to the gym.

When you find it difficult to change your thought pattern, change your body and how it is moving at that moment, and you will then find it easier to change how you are thinking. Exercise is great because it gets those natural endorphins flowing, those happy endorphins which make you smile. That is the state you want to be in most days.

Your main goal in life should be to feel good now, every day. Will you have down moments? Yes you will, but they won't last long, certainly not long enough to change your thought patterns.

What else can help you to be happy now? Like I keep saying, every morning start your day with a five-minute session of gratitude. This is another secret of success. Go somewhere quiet and start to think about all the things in your life that you are grateful for. It may be your spouse, your children, your parents, your job, your lifestyle, whatever you are grateful for. Don't just think about it, feel the feelings of gratitude, let those feelings well up inside of you. This will put your body in a good state, and you will have positive energy before you head off to work. Once you get in a pattern of doing this for five minutes daily, then you can do it at different times throughout the day.

If you notice that you are not feeling good at some point during the day, go somewhere quiet or even just sit at your desk and let those feelings of gratitude take hold of you. You will be realigning yourself. Often the tyres on our cars are not in alignment and we need to get them realigned correctly so our drive is smooth and our tyres wear out evenly. Throughout the day, our thinking often needs some realignment, and a quick session of gratitude can realign us.

Another thing you should do, which we will talk more about in this book, is to have your specific life goal clear in your mind.

In the morning, spend another five minutes and think about that specific goal you have and feel the feelings of already having it, already reaching that goal. How does that feel? Feel that now, feel as if you are already there. Again, feel good now, visualise and act as if you have now what it is that you want in the future.

We spoke previously about writing down on a card the thing that you want in your life and then carrying the card around with you wherever you go. When you are not feeling good, that is the time when you need to get the card out, read what's on it, and visualise already having achieved it. If you become what you think about, then taking control of your thinking throughout the day is extremely important.

Feeling good now is not just about focusing on what you want in the future, it is about the now. Enjoy where you are now while you continue the journey towards what you want. Remember that success is both a journey and a destination.

There are some good things happening in your life, I'm sure. Don't worry about the fact that you don't get the things you want right away. The universe does not work that way, instant gratification is not how it operates. When we plant a seed in the ground, the universe makes us wait until the seed grows into a fruit so we can eat it.

You must get your pattern of thinking and your belief system rooted deep in your subconscious mind and then what you want will come somehow. You will notice little things start to happen that will give you the faith to get you on your way to getting what you want.

On this journey, eagerly anticipate the future while still being happy where you are now. Don't be impatient, because that means that you are thinking about not achieving your goal and that is thinking about lack and, since thoughts become things, if you think of lack then you will get lack.

Feeling good now also means that you look for the good in the bad. If things are happening that are out of your control, then look for the good in them.

Viktor Frankl, a Holocaust survivor, said that between stimulus and response there is a space and in that space we have the freedom to choose our response. So, even if bad things are happening around you, you still have that last human freedom to choose how you will respond to what is happening, and that can be to look for the good in the bad so you can continue to feel good now. Don't focus on the bad because, as the saying goes, where focus goes energy flows. If we continue to think of the things we don't want, these are the things we will continue to get.

Success is not about genetics, bloodline, where we live, what age we are, or what gender we are. Success is simple and, I keep saying this repeatedly, you become what you think about. That is the secret of success. It seems simple but not many people do it, not many people have control over their thinking and that is why it remains a secret. Remember, whatever you really really want, you will get, and whatever you really really don't want, you will get that too.

You cannot focus on the absence of what you want and at the same time expect it to come your way. Every thought must be in the now; you have it now, you are there now. This is what will get into your subconscious mind, and it will affect your entire body. The subconscious mind will believe anything that you continually tell it, if you are in the now when you think about it and when you feel it and if you believe it consciously.

Don't worry about what you see in front of you. If you want more money and all you see is your debt, then debt is all you will get. You may say, the fact is I am in debt. Well, I heard a saying once that, when the attitude is right, the facts don't count. Yes, you may have debt but don't think about it. Take a few moments and set up a payment plan with all your debt and leave it at that and don't give it any more thought. Just focus on having plenty of money.

I used to say many years ago when speaking about people who had money, that it is easy to be stress-free and carefree and happy when you have money. But what I realised is that the money doesn't give you the attitude, the attitude gives you the money. The money will come and the debt will be gone if your attitude and thinking are right on a consistent basis.

When thoughts do not become things is when you cannot believe that you will have what you want. Thoughts become things because you believe that it is possible for you to have them, so start thinking about small things and build up to bigger things. You can have big dreams, but make sure that the next logical step is what you can focus all your energy and thinking on, and that you also believe it can be achieved while you are on your way to the big goal of your life.

As you go through the process of realising that your thoughts do control your world and setting achievable big goals, how do you know if you are on track? Simple – how do you feel? If you feel bad, you are off track and you will have to work out why. Is it that your goal is too big and you don't believe it and that is why you are feeling bad? Have you stopped doing the daily disciplines like gratitude and visualisation and let negative thoughts set in? Is what you want so specific that it is one of a kind and there are many other people who want that one thing? Analyse why you are off track and correct it, and you will know that you have corrected it by the way you feel. If you feel good, you are back on track.

At what level do you believe that you attract things into your life? This is a personal decision. Yes, you become what you think about, but at what level?

As you study how the universe works in a greater way, it will start to become clear to you that everything is energy and that we are all connected. One thing important to remember is that your subconscious mind plays a big role in universal success, so make sure it is programmed for success.

Success is just one decision away. Once you truly make a dedicated decision that you will reach your goal or die trying, then success is what you will have and you will get the very thing that you are after.

It is the law of the universe that you become what you think about.

FIVE

A while ago, there was a young lady who was part of a group I was involved with. She heard from others in the group that she should have really big goals for her life. She seemed to be doing well financially, earning around fifteen thousand dollars a month in income. When people told her to set big goals for herself, her question to the group was whether she should go from earning fifteen thousand dollars a month to now focusing on earning one million dollars a month? I sat back and watched the reaction of the others to this question. The ones who responded to her were all starting off in the personal development field and most had just started setting goals themselves. I was surprised to see that most of the people were encouraging her to set this huge goal for herself, to go from fifteen thousand dollars a month to focusing on earning one million dollars a month of income.

I couldn't believe it, because I knew if this was her goal, she would never reach it. She was jumping too far. Big goals are great, but I just knew that this lady could never believe that she could go from fifteen thousand dollars a month to a million dollars a month because belief is the key.

I did offer a suggestion that was not taken well. My suggestion was, why not set a goal that you can believe in? I said why not go from fifteen thousand dollars a month to fifty thousand dollars a month and then when you reach fifty thousand dollars a month, why not double it to one hundred thousand dollars a month and just keep doubling it when she reaches each goal? Why go for such a big figure when you have to reach the other figures first? I am sure she could get excited about earning fifty thousand dollars a month but no, she wanted to focus on a million dollars a month, and if she continues to focus on that, I can almost guarantee that she will never even come close to it because auto-suggestion is all about belief.

As I said earlier, you have to feel the feelings of already having what you want. This young lady had no idea what one million dollars a month in income feels like, so how could she feel those feelings that she has never come close to? But if the next step was from fifteen thousand dollars a month to fifty thousand dollars a month, then she probably could feel what that would feel like. There are certain thoughts that we don't have access to. We can't access them if those thoughts are too far from what we normally think.

Auto-suggestion plays a big role in our success. Auto-suggestion is when your conscious mind makes suggestions to your subconscious mind and this then leads to how you think and ultimately who you will become. This then will allow you to see the things around you that will lead you to your success and also attract things, people, or circumstances into your life that will lead you to universal success.

Electricity makes the world work and serves mankind so we can stretch human capabilities, but if electricity is used wrongly it can cause the death of humans. Similarly, auto-suggestion can lead you to the top of the mountain of success and a life of peace and prosperity or, if used incorrectly, it can throw you down into the valley of misery and despair. It is all about how you use it. Everyone is using auto-suggestion in their lives whether they know it or not.

There are four ways to look at this, four types of people. The first type is unconsciously incompetent. This person is unaware that they are incompetent. That means that they are unaware of why they are getting all the bad things that they don't want in their lives.

The second person is the one who is consciously incompetent. This person is aware of his incompetence. He knows what he is doing is not working and he is conscious of his incompetence.

The third person is the one who is conscious of his competence. This one knows that what he is doing is working and he continues to do it. He is conscious of his competence.

The last person is unconsciously competent. Two sub-types come under this category. There is someone who does not know what they are doing but it's working, so they are competent at it. They are unconscious of their competence. Then there is the person who for a long time was consciously competent, knew what they were doing, and got the results they wanted. But this type gets to the point where they have been doing it for so long that it just becomes natural for them and they have become unconscious of their competence.

Most people are unconsciously incompetent when it comes to using auto-suggestion to improve their lives. They are influencing their subconscious minds with negativity about how things never work out for them.

The first thing they should try is to become the second type and start becoming conscious of their incompetence, to realise that what they have been doing and thinking up until now has not been working. This is a good place to start because at this point they can start making the needed changes.

The point they should want to get to is where they are conscious of their competence and practise this for a long time, to get to the point eventually where they don't need to consciously think about it anymore and they just naturally attract success into their lives because they have practised auto-suggestion for a long time.

If you fill your mind with doubt and unbelief in your ability to achieve the goals that you have for your life, then this principle of auto-suggestion grabs hold of that unbelief and influences the subconscious mind. This then becomes your dominating thought and this dominating thought draws you towards failure.

Auto-suggestion works with either belief or disbelief.

Your subconscious mind will believe any suggestion that you give it. The results will be either good or bad. The good thing is that you have the power to choose what results you will get with auto-suggestion.

If you fill your mind with a lack of confidence in your own abilities, then you will not be confident and when a challenge arises you will not be able to overcome it. But if you fill your mind with radiant thoughts of confidence, then auto-suggestion makes that your dominating thought and when challenges come your way you will master them and reach the top of the mountain of success.

Self-confidence leads to belief and self-confidence is something that many people struggle with. They may be confident in doing the little things in their life that they do repeatedly, but they have a lack of confidence when it comes to believing that they can be, do, or have anything in their life.

How is your confidence level? What are you feeding your subconscious mind with? If you have a dominating thought of a lack of confidence, then to make confidence a dominating thought you need to build up your confidence level one brick at a time.

You have the power and ability to achieve great things because, if one person can do the thing you want to do, then you can do it as well. You have to start laying down one brick of confidence at a time.

When you do something that requires you to show a little confidence, write it down, reflect on it. Think over your past and remember the big things that you did and reflect on them and keep laying those bricks of confidence. Tell yourself repeatedly that you can do it, that you have the ability. Bet on yourself to win. Start small and then go big. Each brick of confidence laid will eventually build a tower of confidence. One step at a time, one brick at a time.

The most important thing is what you tell yourself. Write down an affirmation in the positive. Something like, *I am so happy and grateful now that I have the confidence to achieve the goals I set for myself and I have the confidence to overcome any challenge that presents itself.* Read this statement day and night and, while you read, feel the feelings of having the confidence that you are seeking.

Auto-suggestion is so powerful. Your self-talk is what will create your world. Extremely successful people do not stumble upon success out of the blue. No, they continue to believe that they can reach the top of the mountain of success and then that belief attracts everything and everyone into their life needed to help them reach their goals.

I will repeat myself again, you are powerful because you are a human being. You have so much energy inside of you that you can be, do, or have whatever you want. Just start with your belief. Start with auto-suggestion.

Always be aware of your self-talk. Be aware of what you are telling yourself. Never allow anything negative to gain entrance through the door of your mind. Keep a guard at that door and let nothing in that won't build you up.

Without using auto-suggestion in a positive way, you are just flipping a coin to determine if you will live the life that you want to live, and for most people that coin lands on the side of failure because if you are not actively thinking of success, your default will go to thinking negatively that you can't do it because that is what is abundant in society today.

Don't be that way. Feel the feelings of already having the things that you want. Set big goals for yourself but make sure the thing that you focus on, the next logical step, is something that is in the realm of possible belief for you. You can be in control of your thoughts if you want to be. They don't ever have to be out of your control again.

Be the captain of your ship, be the one who has had enough of uncontrolled thoughts, and you will be amazed at the changes in your life and the success that comes your way.

SIX

In 1983, a 61-year-old potato farmer named Cliff Young entered the Westfield Sydney to Melbourne Ultramarathon race in Australia. Cliff grew up on a large farm and his family was not well off. They owned around two thousand sheep and oftentimes Cliff, as a young boy, chased the sheep on foot because his family could not afford horses.

As an adult, because of his stamina and fitness, Cliff had a clear goal and that was to win the Sydney to Melbourne Ultramarathon. He didn't want to win it for the prize money, because he had no idea there even was any prize money. No, Cliff just wanted to do it for himself. The race was run over a distance of 875 kilometres (544 miles).

Cliff had told the media before the race that, even at the age 61, he knew that he could run this long-distance race and make it to the end. He knew this because sometimes he would run for days in gumboots rounding up his sheep. Therefore, he knew that if he took it slow and steady, he could make it. He would use a technique that was later dubbed the 'Cliff Young shuffle'.

Cliff turned up on the day of the race in his overalls

and workboots. The other runners who arrived in their running gear thought there was no way that Cliff could finish this ultramarathon. The race started and Cliff fell towards the back of the pack. At the end of the first day, all the other contestants stopped to sleep for six hours before continuing with the race. Whether or not Cliff knew that this was what runners normally did, he didn't stop. Cliff just kept on running. During the night, Cliff took the lead and he just kept running. He eventually won the ultramarathon by ten hours, breaking all the records.

During the race, Cliff imagined that he was trying to outrun a storm in time to get his sheep rounded up. The race took him five days, fifteen hours, and four minutes to complete. This was two days faster than any previous record.

Cliff was awarded the prize money, which he was surprised was being offered. He decided not to take the money, but instead to split it up between the other five runners who finished the race.

Cliff Young had a goal that he believed in. It was a clear goal and he really wanted to achieve it.

Everyone has goals in their life but unfortunately most people have goals that are very small. Often, they don't even realise that they have goals. They have goals to get enough money to pay the bills, get enough money to pay the rent, and many other small goals like those. They are goals, but if that is all that is getting you out of bed in the morning, paying the lousy bills, then that is not enough to effect any real change in your life.

The Art of Universal Success

To get whatever you want in life, there needs to be a burning desire. Something that you really want, because if you want it but it is not something that gets you out of bed in the morning, then achieving it will be hard. You can be, do, or have anything in life, as long as the thing that you want, you want with all your heart.

Some people have so many goals that they can't focus on any of them. They get a vision board and put lots of pictures up of all the things that they want, and they don't focus on any of them because there are too many to focus on. There are others who have goals that they are not excited about.

I ask people this question – What do you want? To reach a goal, it needs to be clear in your mind first, because if you are not clear on the goal, then how will you ever attain it?

What gets you excited? What could get you out of bed early in the morning until late at night. What would it be for you? Is it a romantic loving relationship that you want? Is it to buy a home for yourself and your family? Is it to start your own business? Is it to learn a musical instrument so one day you can play it professionally? Is it like Cliff Young, to finish an ultramarathon or even just a marathon? Do you want to be a millionaire? Do you want to invest in companies? Do you want to travel the world full-time? Do you want to touch the walls of the Colosseum in Rome? Do you want to buy an expensive car or go on holiday to an expensive island? Do you have a goal to fly business class every time you travel? Is your goal that you want to shift overseas or maybe learn another language?

The goal can be anything, as long as you really want it and you believe that you can have it. In my other books, I talk about having goals in different areas of your life, like financial goals, spiritual goals, health goals, or travel goals. But, in this book, we will just pinpoint one specific goal that would do it for you and that you can focus on.

Take a few moments and think of your dream life. Get a pen and paper out and write out your story, the story of what you want your life to be like. This can be a fun exercise. Let your mind wander and see what excites you.

You see, most people are going nowhere. Like I said, they are not living eighty years, they are living one year eighty times. They don't have a vision of the future for themselves. They are vague on what they want and if they have no destination, then they will never go anywhere. Most are like a ship on the high seas without its sails up. The wind and the waves blow it around and it goes in all directions and never reaches anything but the rocks. If the ship had a destination, then it would make sure that its sails were up and in the right position for the prevailing wind so it could head in the right direction. Then it wouldn't matter what wind blows, the ship would stay on course until the destination.

Setting goals is like choosing a destination and then, when life throws all kinds of winds in your direction, then that's OK because you know where you are going and you know that you will get there. Don't be like most people, have a clear destination for your life.

So, have you got your goal clear in your mind and do you believe that you will get there? When people set goals, many set goals that are so big that they don't really believe them. Like I said earlier in discussing the subconscious mind, people may have set a big goal but still not changed their belief system to get them to where they want to go.

Act now as if you are already there. You need to feel the feelings of having already reached your goals. I have said it many times because it is so important to understand. The secret is your belief system. How can you feel the feelings of something that you have never come close to feeling? If you are earning one hundred thousand dollars a year and I said to you to have the feelings of earning one hundred thousand dollars a year, you would say that that was easy to do because you know how it feels because that is what you are earning now. But if you set a goal that is so far out of your belief system, how can you feel those feelings when you have never before come close to feeling that way?

Set goals that excite you but also that you can believe in. If you are earning fifty thousand dollars a year now, why not set a goal to earn one hundred thousand dollars a year? You see, you can believe that, you can feel the feelings of that amount now before you reach it, and that is why you can reach it.

You can have one million dollars a year of income as

a goal in your mind, but you also need to focus on the next logical step and then feel those feelings. Then, when you reach one hundred thousand dollars a year, why not go for two hundred thousand dollars a year? You can get excited about that amount. You have to pass that to get to one million dollars, so why not set that as a goal that your subconscious mind can believe.

The same applies to relationships. If you are all alone and very lonely and depressed and you have never been in a relationship before, how do you know what it feels like to be married to someone you love and who loves you. How would you know what it feels like to have a nice big house with lots of kids? You don't know what that would feel like, so how could you generate those feelings? In that case, why not make your main goal finding a partner whom you can love and who can love you? Start with that and then you can think long-term about a family and the other things.

It is the same with a business. If people tell you to set a massive goal to have your own business with fifty staff members and right now you are an employee stacking shelves, that is too big a goal for you right now. It can be in your mind as the goal you will eventually reach, but you need to focus on the next logical step. Why not set a goal of having your own business where you work for yourself, just you, with no other employees right now? Then you can set a goal to have one employee. Then your next goal can be to have five employees. You can get excited about those goals and you can also feel the feelings of already having achieved them because they are not too far from where you are now.

I cringe when I hear people tell others to set ridiculous goals that they just could never believe in. They will stay broke forever, and most do.

I use the doubling formula when it comes to money. If you want more money, then just keep doubling it. If you are earning two thousand dollars a month, the next goal can be four thousand dollars a month. Then the next goal can be eight thousand dollars a month. You can have a much higher figure in your mind as your ultimate goal, but these smaller amounts are what can be the logical steps to get you to that big amount.

You can still get excited about it when you are doubling it and, as you get higher, then your thinking continues to go higher. If you are earning five million dollars a year now, then doubling that would be fine and believable, but if you are earning one hundred thousand dollars a year now, then making ten million dollars a year your next logical step would not work. You can set that goal if you like but if I was you, I wouldn't.

As you can see, I have again used money as the example because it is easy to quantify, but the process is the same with whatever it is that you want in your life.

I don't want you to think I am promoting wealth. Your life choices are yours, but what I do recommend is to earn as much as you can in the time allotted for work. If you have decided to work thirty hours a week, then make sure you are earning as much as you can for each of those hours. Time is precious. Don't give it away for a low price. You can always earn more money, but you cannot get more time.

People often try to skip steps in life. If you needed to cross a river and there was a series of boulders in the water leading from one side of the river to the other, what would you do? Would you not go from one boulder to the next? Similarly, it's hard to think about earning one million dollars a month when you are behind on your bills and the creditors are calling.

The most important thing is to be clear about the thing that you want. If you are not sure of what to do with your career or what you want for your life, then do what I did years ago when it comes to earning money. A goal I set years ago, and I still update it as I reach it, is to choose the lifestyle I want to live. That is the goal. I choose what style of life I want to live and what I want to do that brings me great joy and then I just set a monetary amount that I need to earn every month so I can live that lifestyle. That is why I was never stuck on the 'how' part of the goal. How will I get what I want? I wasn't smart enough to see what the vehicle would be to get me to the amount I wanted to earn so I could live the lifestyle I wanted.

This maybe something that you can do. A monetary amount is good because it is clear and easy to define, whereas other goals are harder to define. The good thing about money, is that it is everywhere, it is abundant in the world. Money is very important. The need for it is up there with oxygen. You cannot live without earning money somehow. Even if you owned your property and lived off the land and used your own water and didn't use electricity, is some lands the government would still ask you for money every year as a tax for the land. If this is not the case in your country, it would still be difficult to live without money. Money is important and it is serious. If you choose a specific amount, then use the goal card method. Get a card and write on it in the positive about the clear goal that you have in mind.

Let's say that your goal is to earn fifteen thousand dollars a month. You could write on the card, *I am so happy and grateful now that I am receiving fifteen thousand dollars a month so I can now…* and then fill in the rest. Carry this card with you and read it throughout the day. You will find that sometimes during the day your hand will go in your pocket, and you will feel your card and that phrase will automatically leave an imprint on your mind. Doing this will help you keep the goal clear in your mind. You start to believe that you can have it and you start to vibrate those feelings and they will be imprinted on your subconscious mind.

How long will it take for you to reach your goal? It is hard to say because everyone is different and people come from different backgrounds, and they have different belief systems that they need to change. Like I mentioned earlier, one sign that you are on your way is that you feel good. As long as you are feeling good, then you are on your way to achieving your goal. If you start not to feel good, analyse your daily success habits and see if you have stopped those habits that you once started, and then get back on track doing them until you feel good again. You will never get what you want when you are feeling bad. Impatience puts you in a negative vibration state and you start to distance yourself from what you want in life, so don't be impatient.

As long as you are feeling good now, then it is working. The Chinese bamboo tree is a good metaphor for goal setting. The seeds of the tree are planted and farmers water and fertilise them regularly. After a few months of this, they still see nothing growing out of the ground, but they continue to fertilise it and water it. After a year, they see no tree. After four years, they still see no tree. In the fifth year, the tree finally shoots up and in six weeks it grows ninety feet. The farmers could not see any growth with the naked eye, but under the soil there was plenty of movement. If they stopped watering and fertilising the soil at any time, the tree would never have appeared.

So, as long as you are continuing your daily success habits and feeling good now, then you are watering and fertilising your goal and one day it will appear in your life.

Trust the universe that, if you do your part, it will do its part. Have a clear goal in mind, believe that you can have it, continue every day the successful habits that will make the difference in your life, and you will attain the life that you have always wanted.

SEVEN

An African proverb says that if there is no enemy within, then the enemy outside can do you no harm.

There is someone even more dangerous, more destructive, more sinister and worrying for a King and his army than the approaching enemy army that is close to the King's battlelines. The enemy approaching the King might be fearsome and powerful, but this other enemy can do as much if not more harm to the King than the approaching army.

This dangerous person is the enemy behind the lines, the enemy that may be in the midst of the King's camp, lying, cheating, spying, waiting to bring ruin to the King's army. It's this enemy who lays behind the lines who can do the most damage. This enemy could ruin the King's plans. He could sabotage the equipment. He could whisper falsehoods and mistrust in the soldiers' ears. He could feed the army outside with the King's battle plans. He could even kill the King and leave his army without leadership and without hope.

This enemy behind the lines can be devastating to a King and his army.

The King will go to great lengths to find who this spy is because he knows that if he does not find him and deal with him, then he will have to fight the battle on two fronts and he will surely lose.

Today, this enemy lives among us. This enemy is just as insidious as a spy in the King's army. This enemy resides in the minds of most people living today, and I say most people because that is the truth.

Who is this enemy? It is self-worthlessness. In some people it is mild and in others it is extreme. In some, this self-worthlessness can be devastating. This enemy can prevent some people from even getting out of bed in the morning and, for others, this enemy is always within them, whispering untruths in their ear. Things like – you are not good enough, you can't do it, other people can do it but you can't, you are not worthy of happiness, and you are not worthy of success.

This consistent attack within can bring a person to ruin. This person may have goals and dreams, but they will never reach them as long as this enemy is still behind the lines. This person could try all the success techniques that are out there, things like meditation, visualisation, manifestation, but they won't work because that little voice that says that they are not good enough whispers gently and consistently in the person's ear, so all that good work, that time they set aside to practise success habits, was to no avail. That is why so many people say that they are practising all the success habits but are getting nowhere with their goals. One of the reasons is the blocking that is self-worthlessness or lack of confidence. This is what is putting a stop to universal success.

How about you? How strong is this enemy behind the lines in your mind? Are the whispers loud and overwhelming or are they little whispers that pop up in your mind at different times during the day?

If this enemy was a real person and he followed you around all day, standing just behind you whispering untruths like you are not good enough, you can't do it, you have no talent, or you cannot be successful, would you not call the police and get a restraining order on this person? This person may not be physically hurting you, but he would be emotionally hurting you, which can be just as bad.

If you went out for drinks with your friends, and your friend started randomly telling you that you were worthless, you can't reach your goals, you're not smart enough to succeed, and so forth. How many seconds would it take for you to get up and walk out the door – two, three, maybe five seconds?

You see, this is why the enemy within, the enemy behind the lines, is so vicious and powerful. It is hard to walk away from this enemy. You cannot just change locations, because this enemy is always with you.

The good news is that you can win against this enemy, it is a fight that you must be victorious in to truly be successful in life. One of the most important things to remember is this. You have the power to overcome this enemy and to banish him forever. It won't happen in one day, but once you start to discover your self-worth, you will start to soar and you will be done with this enemy once and for all.

No one can make you feel worthless, unless you allow them to do so, knowingly or unknowingly. This is very important to understand because somehow you have allowed this voice to be there in your mind. For most people, they don't even realise that the enemy is there, showing how insidious this voice is.

You have the power and ability to rid yourself of this enemy; you just need to start with a burning desire to be done with him once and for all. The power to do this may be weak at the moment but, like a muscle, the more you work it, the more it will grow and the stronger you will become, and one day there will be no enemy behind the lines, no voice whispering those nasty things into your ear. All that will be left is a voice that is on your side, a voice telling you that you can do it, that you are smart enough, that you have value, and that you can reach your goals and live your dream life.

One thing that can fuel this enemy is starting to think of why we cannot do something and then backing that up with experiences from our past and the times where we may have failed and where we thought that we were not good enough. Times when maybe our friends, our family members, said that we were not good enough to do something, and we then consistently think about that. This just reinforces the thoughts and feelings of worthlessness.

One of the major ways to overcome this type of thinking is to flip it. To think of the times of when you have succeeded and when you were good enough to do a particular thing. The challenges that you overcame, the situations that you handled. The kindness you once showed, the helpless person you took under your wing and helped.

These are the thoughts that you need to consistently hold onto, and when you start to control the way you think, then whenever a negative voice says that you cannot do something because you are worthless, you can turn around to that voice and tell it – I am not worthless, I am a worthy person, I have the ability to accomplish great things, I am perfectly made, I am special. You, little voice, will try and tell me that I can't do it, but I know that you are from my past and have no place in my future. Yes, you are a powerful little voice, but you have no say regarding me today, you have no hold over what I can or cannot do. I am the captain of my ship and I will conquer you, so go away little voice, burrow into the ears of another helpless victim, because you are no longer welcome in my mind. I have tolerated your negative ways for far too long and now, today, I banish you forever. Be gone, little voice and never return until the end of time!

You have the power to tell that voice to go away, even if it returns over and over again. Just keep saying, go away. In scripture, Christ told the Devil to go away, and the Devil did. You can do the same.

Instead of entertaining this negative voice that you

have banished, welcome in the little voice that encourages you, the voice that says that you can do it and that you are not worthless.

Welcome that comforting voice. Say to it, welcome my friend, I know that you care for me because you always encourage me, you always say to me that I can accomplish great things. I thank you my little friend, you are a refreshing voice in a troubled world and I know that even when storms come, and come they will, you will be there right beside me whispering words like, you can do it, you are worthy, you are special, you have great value, and you can accomplish great things, and I know that with you whispering such things in my ear together we will overcome any storm, any powers that be which would do us harm, anybody who tries to drive negative thoughts deep into my mind, because you are a true companion who is whispering truths in my ear, and for this I thank you. My mind is now your permanent home, and I am in awe of the amazing things we will accomplish together.

Take a moment and think about your body. Not the body on the outside, but on the inside. How you are made, how everything works. It is absolutely marvellous. Not even the smartest human on Earth knows how to create a little part of it, like a finger. We can go to the Moon, but we cannot create any part of the human body. You are magnificent and you must continue to reassure yourself of this.

Think of your mind, think of how you can love and care for another. The comfort that you can give others, only humans can provide. All other creatures just live their lives following instincts, without self-awareness, but you and I are different. So, you have every reason to think that you are worth that much because of who you are, what you can do, and where you can go.

Reassure yourself of this daily. Spend a few minutes at different times of the day and appreciate yourself, override any thinking that you may have been raised with, any thinking that you may have been brainwashed with, intentionally or unintentionally. The thinking like – you are nothing and you are worthless. You may never have heard negative words like these as you were growing up, but sometimes we can think that others close to us may think these things about us, and then we make that thought a reality by constantly thinking about it. We breathe life into the negative seed that we may have accidentally implanted into our mind.

You have the ability to change that. You can start now. You can start to think differently today. I am not saying that change will happen overnight, but if you start today to banish any thoughts that make you feel worthless and replace them with thoughts that make you feel worthy and valuable, then each day you will stack up bricks of worthiness and as the weeks and the months go by, you will start to love yourself, so that is exactly what you should start to do.

Love yourself, not in an arrogant way thinking that you are better than other people, but in a way where you know that you are special. What gift could you ever receive in this world that would compare to existence, what would compare to who you are and how you are made? Absolutely nothing, so you have every reason to love yourself.

Don't be sold on people saying that there is a quick fix to feelings of self-worthlessness. It's not true. If you have thought that you are not good enough for years, you won't change that in a few days because it most likely is embedded in your subconscious mind. The only way to change what is in the subconscious mind is to start to change what messages you feed to that part of the mind. If you change to thinking that you are worthy, as we just discussed, those thoughts will seep into your subconscious mind and filter out all the negative thoughts that have been in there for years.

The good thing is that positive thoughts are much more powerful than negative thoughts, so even if it took you years to develop a pattern of thinking that you are worthless, it won't take you the same time to start thinking that you are worthy and that you are special, nowhere even close to the same amount of time, because of the impact and effect of positive thoughts.

What is good is that, if you start now, as the days go on you will see a big change and you will start to feel great and feel confident and then in time it will be concreted into your subconscious mind. The effect can be felt early, as long as you have banished that negative whisper, that enemy in your ear, and have replaced it with a positive whisper, a friend that will now carry on with you through the journey of life.

Imagine how the King would feel once he discovered who the enemy hiding behind his line was and got rid of him. Think of the relief that the King would now feel to know that behind the line there was security and no one trying to undermine his efforts. The King no longer has to focus on this problem, and all his attention can now be focused on the enemy army approaching his line. The insidious threat is over, he now has control of his army and the confidence to move forward in his conquests.

That will be the same with you.

Be careful of the people whom you associate with regularly. You may banish that little negative voice from inside of you, but if there is a negative voice from outside, from people you spend time with, then it will be hard to counteract that with your positive thinking.

Spend time with those who have banished this little voice of worthlessness from their minds; these are the ones to give a lot of your time to. Go where they go, read what they read, and talk like they talk, because you will become just like them. Walk away from those who whisper unkind words to you and from those who try knowingly or unknowingly to implant negative thoughts in your mind. These people will keep you down, keep you unsuccessful and living a life just like them. Don't be that way; walk away and choose your friends and your associates wisely.

Make a commitment to yourself that you will banish negative voices forever. When you do this, you will find peace and contentment. You will be able to be alone with your mind, because it will now be on your side.

Remember that the universe is on your side on your journey to becoming a person who understands your own value. The journey can be an easy one or a hard one; it is up to you. If you decide that it will be easy, then that is what it will be, but if you decide it will be hard then that too is what it will be. It doesn't need to be hard; it can be a great journey that you can enjoy.

Be grateful every day for your existence, feel the feelings of gratitude. You can feel contentment in knowing that your most dangerous enemy is no longer there. You will realise that you can handle any enemy on the outside because the enemy inside is now gone, and then you can be free to pursue your dreams of a successful life with the contentment of knowing that you are special and worthy of a happy life.

You will have the confidence to overcome anything that life throws at you and now, instead of being the one needing help and support, you will be in a position to offer help and support to the needy one and the helpless one, and the joy that will come from that will make sure that that negative voice is banished for all time.

EIGHT

Once upon a time, there was a Persian merchant who was travelling the sandy dunes looking for a place to rest. He arrived in the city of Tehran and proceeded to inquire in the city for a new servant. After a while, a new servant was presented to the merchant. What the merchant did not know was that this servant was running away from a murder he had committed.

A few weeks later, while resting in his tent outside the city, the merchant asked his servant to go into the marketplace and buy some provisions, so the servant went off. After a little while, the servant returned to his master trembling with fear. The master noticed the pale look on his servant's face and asked what was wrong. The servant replied, "Just now while I was in the marketplace a woman brushed me while walking past. I turned to see who this woman was and I began to tremble, for the woman I saw was Death. She looked at me with a surprising, piercing glance that sent shockwaves through my body. So please, Master, lend me a horse and let me ride to Samara to flee from her." The master agreed and gave his servant a horse on which the servant galloped off to Samara.

The merchant decided to go into the marketplace to find this woman, Death. When the master found her, he asked her why she put so much fear into the heart of his servant. Death said that she did not mean to scare the man's servant. She was just astonished to see the servant here in Tehran, because she had an appointment to meet him tonight in Samara.

This story is a tale of fate. I tell it despite not believing in fate, or in destiny. I don't believe that we are destined from birth to do certain things in life. I believe we create our own destiny. I am sure that you would not like someone else to write your life story for you. I would like to think that you want to create your future and not be a robot just following your programming. If you believe in fate, then that is your choice. I am not here to detract from what you believe in. We each have choices about what we believe.

I just find it hard to believe that someone in one part of the world is destined to be rich, while another person in another part of the world is destined for starvation. The sort of fate I do believe in, and the reason I told you this tale, is the law of sowing and reaping. It is not fate as such, it is the law that there are consequences to every decision that you make, good or bad. This is the sort of fate that you cannot jump on a horse and flee from, because it will always meet you somewhere and oftentimes it is somewhere you do not expect it to be. Whatever we do in our lives, good or bad, there is an effect and the consequences always return to us without fail.

If you are a farmer and you plant carrot seeds, will you ever get potatoes from those seeds? No, of course not. You will always get carrots from carrot seeds. Whatever the farmer plants, waters, and fertilises, that very thing is what the farmer will reap.

This is the same in all our lives. If we plant seeds of negativity, of wrongdoing, misconduct, fraudulent schemes, or law-breaking, then at some point the consequences of our actions will catch up with us. That cannot be avoided.

It is the same with the opposite as well. If we do good things, help people, and are honest in all our dealings, if we think of positive things consistently and are kind to everyone, then we will have good things returned to us no matter where we go. Whether good or bad, the seeds that we plant are what we will get in return.

If we have done some unkind things, but then start to change and turn in the opposite direction, then those consequences may come, but not in a severe way. We may have treated a friend badly but, if we change, we may win that friend back, but we also might not. Maybe the consequence of those bad actions towards your friend is that your friend has more dealings with you. If that is the case, then that is a more acceptable consequence of your actions.

What we should do is learn from our mistakes, so we can avoid severe consequences in future, but not try and flee from them. People try and protect themselves from the mistakes they make, but it is not possible. Because consequences are inevitable, they will catch up with you, whether in one city or the next. You can try, but each of us must deal with reaping whatever we have sown in the past. No one can protect us from our unique fate.

What we all should do is learn from the mistakes of our past and vow never to repeat them. That way, we will plant many more good seeds than the bad seeds we may have planted in the past.

I am sure that many people who have passed away now wished that they had done things differently. Sadly, some have gone to their graves never changing. There are many people in history who I think may have wanted to do things differently had they had the chance. The good thing is, we can learn from the examples of others and not make the same mistakes.

Marcus Crassus lived a time long ago. He was a Roman politician in the time of Julius Caesar and Pompey. Crassus seemed to have had only one focus and that was to make money. Even if it meant doing questionable things, he would do anything to increase his financial status. A once good businessman turned into a greedy politician doing whatever it took to become wealthy.

Crassus formed the fire brigade of Rome, and it is said that when his firemen arrived to put out a fire, they would refuse to do so unless the person who owned the burning building sold it to Crassus for a fraction of what it was worth. This way Crassus was able to acquire a lot of property and add to his wealth.

One day, his greed led him to make a few bad

decisions that led to his death. Crassus had one main mission and that was to fight the Parthians. There was no real reason to go on this particular campaign, but the reason Crassus wanted to fight this battle was that the Parthians were wealthy and, if he could defeat them, he would acquire more wealth for himself. His greed finally led to his death at the Battle of Carrhae against the Parthians. His life was cut short because of this relentless drive for more and more wealth which got out of hand.

Crassus is a good example of what not to be like. Greed is a horrible thing. It takes wanting to make money to the extreme where you start to ignore good values and good deeds in the rush to become wealthy.

I am not promoting poverty and I am also not promoting being wealthy. It is up to each individual how they want to live their lives. It could be a life in the service of others, with little money, or it could be a big business that makes them lots of money so they can do whatever they like with their life. It is up to each person how they will live.

Whatever way of life we choose, the warning is not to be greedy. This warning is for both the poor and the wealthy. Poor people can be just as greedy as wealthy people. Poor people can lie, cheat, and steal to get money, and that is greed, and wealthy people can do the same.

If you have a desire to increase your income, then heed the warning of the life of Marcus Crassus. If not kept in check, the consequences of focusing only on wealth may lead you down a similar path. That doesn't have to happen, it is just a warning which we all need to remember.

We all have only so many working hours in the day. As I have mentioned previously, you should earn as much per hour as you possibly can in the time you have set aside for business. So, for example, if you have set aside thirty hours a week to work, then for each of those hours try to earn as much as you can, so as to improve the value of your work.

Increasing the amount that you want to earn per hour is not being greedy. What you are doing is increasing your value for an hour that you work. You can thus grow and become a better person, more competent, with more experience and more understanding, and you will of course add value to the marketplace.

Many people sacrifice things that are important to them in their quest to become wealthy. It seems that money is the most important thing for them. It is when you want it all, and don't care what you lose in the process, that you become a greedy person.

My teacher said that if he had known the price that he would have to pay to be wealthy, he would never have paid that price. People sacrifice friends, family, spouses, and even their souls because of the desire to be wealthy. Greed is desire out of control. It gets out of control when money starts to drive you, when money starts calling the shots in your life. It led Crassus to rip people off and it led him to his death. Greed was in control there, not the desire to earn more money.

As I keep saying, when it comes to finances, whatever you want to earn is up to you. If you want to increase your finances, then remember what I mentioned earlier about taking one step at a time. People say that you can have anything that you dream of, but that is not true. You can have anything that you *believe* in, that is true.

So, have financial goals and believe that you can attain them. Go one step at a time and get excited about where you are going, and don't sacrifice your loved ones for wealth.

Unfortunately, there have been people throughout history who showed little compassion or concern for others, while at the same time living an extravagant lifestyle.

Somebody who lived this way, from whose life we can learn, was Marie Antoinette, Queen of France.

Marie Antoinette was the last French Queen before the revolution. She was of Austrian descent and was married to King Louis the Sixteenth. She became unpopular with the people of France because of her lavish spending and lifestyle while many people were starving. All she seemed to care about was herself, and a few close friends whom she made wealthy, while the common people suffered.

As Queen, her role was to help lead her people to improvement and prosperity, but unfortunately she did the opposite. It may have been her young age, or it may have been her upbringing in the Austrian royal family, that influenced her to take whatever she wanted while her people starved. Maybe she never viewed the French people as her own, especially as she was married to Louis at only 15.

The people had very little to eat, but it seemed that all Marie Antoinette wanted was to continue her lavish lifestyle. A King and Queen should have what they want in life, after all they are the King and Queen, but not at the expense of their people who are suffering and dying of starvation.

Because of her position, she should have shown more compassion for the French people instead of spending all her time at the Palace of Versailles.

Her uncaring, lavish lifestyle made the people hate her and want to kill her.

Unfortunately, it was a little too late for her and Louis to try and change things because the revolution was about to begin. Once it took hold, the King and Queen were captured. After some time spent in prison, King Louis was beheaded and not too long afterwards, Queen Marie Antoinette also met her end beneath the guillotine's blade. Her child Louis-Charles was mistreated and eventually perished.

What devastating consequences from the seeds that she had sown, of being uncaring, greedy, and unwilling to help when she had the power and influence to do so. She could not escape these consequences. The consequences did not have to be so drastic for her, but in the end she reaped what she had sown. If she had acted differently and influenced her husband to start making some good changes in France, the revolution may have never taken place and she may have died in her old age with her son Louis-Charles as King.

Marie Antoinette is a great example of what not to do, especially when you have the ability, influence, and power to do good. Living a successful, happy life comes with responsibility. If you are successful at whatever you do, you may find that you have influence over people. People who are not yet where you are will look up to you for guidance and support. What will you do when that time comes? What seeds will you sow now and thus reap in future?

Compassion for people who are not where you are in life is the key. Not looking down on the unsuccessful, but helping them up. Not being greedy and building an empire while never lending a hand to the downtrodden. If you make good money, use it wisely and help the needy. Help people become better and never let your success make you feel that you are above everyone else.

I am sure, since you are reading this book, that you will not be that way, but we are all imperfect, me included, and if we are not careful with the trends of our thoughts and our actions, then we might start down a path of greed, lack of compassion, and arrogance.

If we can take these warning examples and learn from them and not even take a step in the direction of these negative qualities, then we will continue to sow seeds of positivity, compassion, and understanding.

Many people are not where you are now or where

you will be. Their life trauma is their own, but if you can sow these good seeds then not only will you be able to help them, but you will also help yourself and when you are older and look back at the life you have lived, you can be proud of the good things that you have done and know it was worth all the time and effort you put in.

NINE

Once upon a time in a big castle lived a King. One day the King called in his jester and asked him to do something for him. He asked the jester to leave the castle and mingle with his subjects in the streets, markets, and taverns. The jester asked why the King was making such a request. The King said that he wanted to know what the people were saying about him, whether good or bad.

The jester, following the King's command, set out and started to mingle with the people in the markets and in the taverns. As the day drew to a close, he returned to the King and reported what he had seen and heard.

The jester told the King that some people did not like him. There were others who liked the King and there were some who neither liked nor disliked him. The King thanked the jester for doing this and said, "It is always good for a king to know what his people are thinking and how they are feeling." The jester asked him, "Why it is good to know these things, for after all, you are the King?" The King responded, "Whenever a soldier goes into battle, he must know what condition his sword is in. He needs to know if his sword is sharp or if it is blunt. Not knowing could mean the end of the soldier's life… Now I know the condition of my sword."

A successful person does well to know what is out there in the world, what the people are doing and what they are saying in the markets and in the taverns, so to speak. To learn how and why people act in different ways all over the world. The King in our story now knows what the people are thinking, and so he can go about his reign in the right way to strengthen his kingdom.

We strengthen our lives, our character, when we travel to distant lands and learn how and why people do things the way they do.

I will talk a little about travel, because a truly successful person becomes well-rounded from travelling and learning how and why people act in particular ways across the other side of the world. Travel can do amazing things for people if they travel wisely. Not just travelling to a distant land to sit on the beach the whole time and then return home. Yes, we do need to rest here and there, but a real traveller uses most of his time to learn about the places that he visits, the cultures he learns about. He seeks to know why people do the things that they do. He learns why they have chosen a particular way of living.

The jester of old had a great position in the royal courts because he was close to the King. He would brighten the day of the King when his master felt a little gloomy. The jester, even though only a servant, was often very intelligent and Kings and Queens valued their company.

The jester was the only one who could give the King bad news and not fear punishment, not fear that the King would kill the messenger. Because of this, the jester could report to the King the things that he heard from the people. He would report how subjects were feeling about their King. The jester spent a lot of time in the markets, the streets, and the taverns. If people thought that the jester was a fool, they would speak openly and the jester could report their opinions to the King.

The travellers of today are like the jesters of old. They leave their home, go out into the world, and see, hear, and learn about how other people act and how they do things differently. They gather all this information, all of this experience, and then they return home and bring it back to their community in hopes that it will enrich the lives of the people in their hometown. The people who don't travel can learn from these travellers and develop an open mind about the rest of the planet's population.

The Venetian explorer Marco Polo, after travelling for decades through Asia, a long way from Venice, said of his story, "I did not write half of what I saw, for I knew that I would not be believed."

The world is an amazing place. Even though we are all human, we can be very different in our thinking and in our actions. As a successful traveller, you don't need to feel that any one way of living is better than another. You can appreciate the differences in people.

In some cultures, family is everything. The whole family has breakfast together and then they head out to work and school and other places. When it is lunchtime, they all return home again to eat together. In the afternoon they head out again to go about their activities. When it is dinnertime, they all return to the dinner table and eat the meal as a family. In other cultures, the family just says goodbye in the morning and then all leave for the day and don't see each other again until the evening.

Some cities in the world are all about no-nonsense business, and in other parts the people are more relaxed and go at life a little slower. City life is different from country life. Mountain life is different from coastal life. All are different and a good traveller will endeavour to discover the differences for himself. He will learn all the different foods that are out there and how some foods will make some people run for the door and other people will see the same food as a delicacy and enjoy it. Some cultures love tea, some love coffee, some love wine, others love spirits. All are different and all are great.

As a person who wants to live a successful life, I ask you to be your local jester and put on a backpack and go on a well-designed travel experience that will enrich you and will also enrich your family and community upon your return.

I will tell you about one place where I spent four weeks and that is Switzerland.

The Swiss alps are one of the most remarkable places I have ever seen. The beauty of the mountains is amazing and what is great about many of these Swiss towns, is that they are so high up in the mountains but still easily accessible by cable car. In other places in the world, to get to the same height and see such amazing views, you would have to climb, but in Switzerland there are many towns high up in the mountains that are easily accessible by lift or cable car.

This is great, not only for the views and the tranquillity of the mountains, but also because you meet people who have lived their whole lives in these little towns high in the alps, some resting right on a cliff's edge. Many families in these hilltop villages go back for generations. One of my favourite little villages high in the alps is named Gimmelwald.

Gimmelwald is a very small village nestled high up on a cliff's edge.

The town has one very small road that goes through it and homes on either side of the road. These people live a peaceful life. They are far away from the hustle and bustle of city life. Yes, they get tourists walking through their town during the day, but they enjoy this because they don't need to travel to discover different cultures around the world; the different cultures come to them. You can spend the night in this village as a guest of local people and discover how they live, how they feed themselves and get all that they need high up there in the mountains.

The great part of travel is when you investigate why these people have decided to live high up in the mountains in peace while others live in the hectic busy cities down below. This is the exciting part of travel which will enrich your life. You can discover for yourself all these beautiful locations, places that may be very different to where you come from. That's travel, that is one of the things that will make you want to travel more and discover things for yourself. Connecting with these people is an experience that you will not forget.

That's the point of it all. People say that most of the world is discovered already but that doesn't matter, when you go and discover it for yourself it will be like no one has discovered it before, because those first feelings are what you will cherish.

There are things that I wish I could see again for the first time. I can't see the Colosseum again for the first time. I can't discover Vernazza in the Cinque Terra of Italy again for the first time. I cannot unsee and then see the beautiful Swiss alps again, but that is ok because the memories and the feelings are still there and when you return home, you can get people excited about the things that you have seen and then they can go out and discover it for themselves for the first time. When you talk about what you have seen, you not only honour the cultures that you have visited, but it will also do something for your character when you talk about what you have experienced and how it has influenced you.

Many people in the world have decided that they don't want to travel. To this you may say – really? Yes, people have personally told me this and I feel sad because I know what they are missing out on.

I was on a walking tour not too long ago in Lucerne,

Switzerland when I met a couple from the USA who retired and have now started to travel. They were excited to be in Switzerland and now wished that they were here earlier in their lives. The gentleman said that finally he is seeing how other people are living and he was excited to learn about my culture and the local culture so he could be influenced.

I am glad that he is travelling now, but if he and his wife had started earlier, the tales, the stories, the experiences that they could have brought back home would have been priceless. However, it is never too late to start and I am sure that now, in their later years, they are doing their best to discover new and exciting cultures around the world.

Never begrudge the time and money you spend travelling far away from your homeland. You cannot put a price on the things you will learn and the fortification of your character. When you travel, you will hear about people who martyred themselves for the cause of freedom under an oppressor. You will learn about people who overthrow a monarchy because they wanted change. You will learn about the after-effects of world war and how it still takes a toll on the people living today. You will learn about families and communities that are trying to hold onto good old traditions while their children are growing up in a world that differs greatly from those traditions.

You will taste the most amazing food and drink the most amazing wine, with great company. You will tell tales of heroes and monsters. You will laugh and you will cry, but in the end you would never want it any other way.

Be a jester, go outside the castle walls and see what is out there. Discover it for yourself and let it enrich your life and then bring back home what you have learned. Tell the stories to your people and, by doing this, you will fortify your character and it will be another building block of a successful life. Don't be surprised if you find that there are things you cannot tell your people about out of fear that they might not believe you.

TEN

Victor Herman was an American born in 1915. Growing up, he found himself in the USSR when the Ford motor company sent his family over to work in their factory in the Soviet Union. As a young man, Herman was a tough kid and so he joined the Soviet Air Force. There he was taught to parachute and he broke the world record for the highest parachute jump. When the authorities asked him to sign the world record certificate, he put USA as his citizenship. He was urged to put USSR and when he refused he was arrested and put into prison for a year. The prison conditions were extreme and terrible, and he was beaten daily. But, because of his tough disposition, he survived his time in prison.

He was later sentenced to ten years in a Siberian *gulag* camp. He survived the extreme conditions, the freezing weather, the beatings, torture, starvation, and the hard labour. Throughout all his time in the camp, he never gave up hope of returning home. In 1976 he was allowed to return home to the country of his birth, the United States of America.

Victor Herman was one of the toughest men who ever

lived. When you study the details of his imprisonment and the strength he needed to show on a regular basis, you will agree that he was one tough man. He never gave up his hope of freedom, and this hope and it alone was his driving force to overcome any challenge.

We may not face these sorts of conditions in our lives, but many do face challenges. It is how you face the challenge which determines whether you will overcome it or not. If you steer into the challenge and have a clear vision of overcoming it, then you will be able to do so.

We don't need to face the same huge challenges as Victor Herman to prove to ourselves that we can overcome big obstacles. We can do it daily over the weeks and months of our life. There are always challenges that pop up, both big and small. The question is, how will you respond? Will you sit in the corner and hide from them or will you be like Victor Herman and look deep within yourself to discover the strength to overcome them?

We all have a Victor Herman inside of us and if we want to live a life of success and happiness, we need to find that person within ourselves so we can overcome every little or big challenge that comes our way.

What if your partner decided to leave you one day and never return? How would you be? What if you lost your job tomorrow? How would you be? If the bank took your home from you? If someone at work said something unkind to you? Whether small challenges or big ones, if we don't overcome them then we remain prisoners in our own lives.

Take a different viewpoint when it comes to these challenges. Look at each situation that arises as a chance to flex your Victor Herman muscles. See each challenge as an opportunity to grow and, if you can handle the small challenges that arise in your life, then you will be in a better position to handle the big challenges which will eventually show their ugly face.

Remove the word 'problem' from your vocabulary. Replace it with 'challenge' or 'situation' because it isn't a problem if you can overcome it and solve it. Even if you can't change the external circumstances, like Victor Herman stuck in the camp, you still have control over your internal circumstances, your mindset, your attitude to what is happening to you, and this is something that no one else has control over.

No one can get their hands on your attitude if you don't allow it. This is the last human freedom that no guard, no official, no person can ever control. Remember that nothing is good and nothing is bad, it is only your thinking that makes it so.

If you can start to control your thoughts, then you can start to overcome whatever challenge you face because the biggest challenges that you will have to overcome in your life are the challenges in your mind, in your thinking. This is the biggest challenge, but once you can get a hold of how you think, you then become the captain of your ship and there is no challenge out there that can defeat you.

As I mentioned earlier, happiness only comes from

within, so even if your partner leaves you it does not need to affect your happiness, because your happiness is from within, not from external circumstances.

Reasons play a big role in overcoming obstacles. Victor Herman had a reason for overcoming his challenges; he looked to the future and so can you.

When challenges arise in your life, focus on your goals, on the next logical step that will get you from where you are to where you want to go, and this focus will have an effect on your thinking. It can affect you in a good way or bad way, it is up to you. It does not need to affect you in a bad way. You don't need to struggle. Life does not need to be hard, because your thoughts are something that you and only you have dominion over, and you can control them.

Is it easy? No, but it is simple. Not easy but simple. It starts with the daily little challenges that we face, no matter how small, which can be little opportunities to grow. I would like you to do something for the next 30 days. Highlight these things that I will now mention and also write them down in a notebook and carry them around with you every day to remind yourself to do them.

For the next 30 days, challenge yourself to do the following things. Some of these things we spoke about earlier, but lock these things in for 30 days.

Every morning when you get up, be grateful for being alive. Be grateful to experience this wonderful gift of existence. It is a precious thing.

Don't turn the news on during the day. If there is something specific that affects the area that you live in, give it a quick look and ignore the rest, and stay positive.

Before you go to work, spend five minutes feeling grateful for life. Go over the things in your life that you are grateful for. I am sure you can come up with some things. Feel the feelings of gratitude; don't just think about them but actually feel them.

Before you leave your house, make sure that the soldier standing guard at the entrance to your mind is awake and alert and lets nothing negative in.

As you go about your day, monitor your thoughts and your feelings. While you monitor them, if you ever start to think of negative things and feel bad, do something to reverse it. Change what you are thinking about or change your state by doing something physical. Keep your goals in mind so you can start to feel good again and this will push out the bad feelings that you have. If you stay in the moment and don't think of the bad that could come or the bad in your past, then you can stay happy and positive because you are in the moment focusing on your goals and keeping them at the forefront of your mind.

When you are on the job, do more than you get paid for. Don't just do the bare minimum at work, go well above what is expected of you daily. Keep getting better every day. It's not just about making the company money, it is knowing that no matter what you do, you do your best at it, and this gives you internal satisfaction that will keep you growing every day.

Let other people leave the lights on when they leave the hotel room, not you. Turn them off, not because of saving power for the hotel but because you are starting to live life at another level. If you drop a little piece of paper on the ground, pick it up and put it in the trash. Don't do it for the government, do it for your development, because you are becoming the best person that you can become.

Throughout the day, smile. Force it if you need to, but smile. Soon you will never have to force it, because there is always something that you can think about that will make you smile. Smile when you greet people. It will improve your mood and improve their mood.

Treat people throughout the day with respect. Even if you don't respect them, still treat them well when you interact with them. Treat them as the most important person in the world because, to them, they are.

As I mentioned earlier, monitor your thinking and feelings throughout the day. If you start to have negative thoughts, push them out of your head with positive thinking. One way to do this is to have your goals clearly in mind.

Whichever goal you have that excites you, a goal you are starting to realise, think about it and this will force negative thoughts out of your mind. It is sometimes not an easy thing to do, but it is worth doing. The only way to stop thinking about pink elephants is to start thinking about blue elephants. The only way to stop thinking about what you don't want is to start thinking about what you do want.

Help people whenever you can. Be the strength that will come to the rescue of those who need help. You are the strength at home, at work, and in your community.

At least once a day, go to a quiet area and sit and visualise the specific thing that you want in your life. Focus on just one thing that is in your sweet spot. The spot where it excites you to have it and you also believe that you can have it. Think about the thing that you want as if you have it already. What would that feel like? Feel the feelings of already having what you desire. It's here, you have it. How would you feel? Then focus on those feelings and know that, if you can think it and believe it, then you can have it.

Thankfulness is such an important aspect of our lives. Just going through the day and saying thank you, thanking your family, your boss, the person who makes you your coffee in the morning, thanking them all. When you walk down the street and see something that pleases you, say thank you. If you believe in a Creator, thank your Creator. When you see a tall, beautiful mountain, say thank you. When you see a rainbow, say thank you. When you feel a warm soft breeze blowing across your body, say thank you.

I was in Fiji once and I arrived at my hotel around dinner time. For dinner, I sat near the water and had a beautiful meal. While I was eating, I was feeling a nice warm island breeze continually passing over me. At the same time, the noise from the gentle waves made me just say thank you. Be thankful for whatever happens throughout your day. It will keep you in a good mood to be grateful for everything in life.

As you close every day, think again about all the things that you were grateful for during that day, even the little things, and as you close your eyes and start to drift off, thank your Creator for life, for existence, and think about the future that is before you. Your sleep will be sweet and productive because these real thoughts with their real feelings will seep into your subconscious mind as you fall asleep.

These are some of the most important things that you can do to live a successful life. I am sure that you want to be successful in everything that you do. You can be successful in business, but that does not necessarily mean that you will be successful in a relationship. You may be a successful traveller, but have no idea how to succeed financially. You could be a successful scientist, but not a successful son or father.

The things I have outlined in this book will help you to be successful in all things because the principles can be applied in every situation.

People think that if they just manifest what they want in life, they will be a success, but that is not always true. If you wanted more money and you got more money, but your personality makes you difficult to get along with or you have a temper and tend to lose control over your emotions, then yes, you were successful at getting the money you wanted, but were you successful in general?

That is where you want to be, no matter what your

focus in life is, what your main goal is. This is universal success, the ability to use your thinking to create your world, not just your immediate goals but all aspects of your life.

When you can start taking control of your thinking and use the universe to help you live a successful life, then you will start to not only have the things that you want but also become the person that you want to be. The loving relationships, the travel, the money, the kindness, the love, the compassion, the understanding, the tolerance. You will be the considerate, the rescuer, the teacher, the poet, the journeyman, the lover, the person living an all-round successful life.

Living this successful life all begins with doing the things that I mentioned before. Not only thinking about the goals you want to achieve, but the daily habits, the gratitude, the visualisation, the positivity, the control over thoughts, the smiles, the respect, the vision, and the journey.

The habits of success cannot be done every now and again; they need to be done daily because each habit done daily is a brick of success in the building of a successful life.

Yes, you can be, do, or have anything that you believe that you can be, do, or have, but if you have a bad personality, bad relationships, a lot of unhappiness, moodiness, or a life of not caring about or understanding people, then even if you have all the money in the world, you won't be living a successful life.

From this day on, go all-out, transform your life, and continue these daily habits so you can live the best life you can live. You will be amazed at who you become when you sincerely practise the habits that we just spoke about. Practise them daily and, not long after you start, you will see changes and seeing these changes will lock you into a lifetime of success.

ELEVEN

Isabella Stewart Gardner was one of America's leading art collectors. She passed away in 1924, but before she died she founded an art museum named after herself in Boston, Massachusetts. In her gallery, she displayed all of her remarkable collection of art from painters like Vermeer, Rembrandt, Degas, and Manet, among others. Her wish was that no pieces from the gallery be sold and that no further pieces be added to the gallery.

Many years after her passing, security at the museum was lax. Not wanting to undertake major renovations because of the founder's wish that nothing be changed, the museum made some small security upgrades but did not secure the museum as well as it could have been.

On Sunday 18th March 1990, there was a break-in. Two men disguised as police officers pulled up to the side entrance of the building and buzzed the guards on the intercom, saying they were there because of a report of a disturbance. The guards didn't know of any such report, but the two men were dressed in police uniforms, so they let them in. It was around 1:30 in the morning.

The two robbers dressed as police officers lured one security guard away from the desk he was sitting at, the only spot where there was a button to call the real police. The fake officers handcuffed both guards and revealed that they were thieves who were there to rob the museum.

They took the guards down to the basement and left them there while they stole artwork worth a fortune. They left the frames and just took the canvases.

The thieves left and the next morning when the next shift came in, all they found was an empty security desk, missing works of art, and two security officers tied up in the basement.

The FBI later valued the haul at about two hundred million dollars and raised the amount to around five hundred million dollars a decade later. The police suspected at first that one of the security guards may have been in on the heist, but could find no real evidence. They then suspected the biggest crime boss in Boston, but once again had no evidence of his involvement.

Years passed and many suspects were ruled out. One man who stood out from the rest was Bobby Donati, a criminal who was murdered a year after the robbery. It was said that he stole the paintings and wanted them to use as leverage to get a friend out of jail early.

For now, no one knows who pulled off the heist. No one has been convicted of the crime. It is still a mystery who dared to steal artwork worth around five hundred million dollars. The frames that held these artworks still hang in the museum empty, in hopes that one day the stolen paintings will be restored to their original places.

These men were thieves, and they did what any thief would do, which is steal. The things that thieves steal are not always expensive. Sometimes a thief will steal because he is a thief and that is just what thieves do. He might steal because the item is valuable, but he also might steal because he doesn't want the owner to have the item. The item itself may mean nothing to the thief and may not be valuable, so the thief can't sell it, but sometimes a thief just steals to take something away from another person.

Unfortunately, on your way to success, you will come across many thieves. Instead of these thieves wanting something tangible, the thing many of these thieves want is your dreams. They steal dreams, they steal the very things that you want. They don't steal them tangibly, but they will steal them by doing and saying things to you that will prevent your dream coming true. Tangible or intangible, it is still theft. Whether they are doing it on purpose or doing it without realising it, they are still thieves. Don't let anyone steal your dreams.

People want you to do well, they just don't want you to do *that* well. They will impose their reality on you and say that you need to be realistic. They will impose their limitations on you and say that you can't succeed.

If someone is not encouraging you to go after your dreams, they may be trying to steal your dreams. This often happens when someone starts on a personal development journey. Their friends don't like that they are changing and, consciously or subconsciously, they put roadblocks in front of their friend who is trying to be successful in what they want to do with their life.

Some may feel that, if their friend improves their life and becomes successful, then they will be left behind, and that scares many people. It scares them because they don't want to be left alone in their misery. Haven't you heard the saying that misery loves company? Although these might be your friends, they are still trying to steal your dreams.

What are some of the things they are stealing from you? They are stealing from your future, things like your future happiness, your car, your future children's education. They are stealing the world trip you have planned. They are stealing your future business, your home, the pool that you want for your home. They are stealing your piano skills, the doctorate in medicine that you would have received years down the track. They are stealing the future songs you will write and perform, your paintings that one day will be called masterpieces. They are stealing your control over your thoughts. They are tearing joy away from you. They are stealing everything you want to do in the future. Don't let them, they are thieves.

They may say that they care for you, but what sort of person who cares for another would not encourage that person to go after their dream life and not be excited as they succeed?

You may tell a friend about a business idea and they may say that it won't work. Wow, what a thief. The thief just came straight out and tried to steal your dream. If you let him steal that dream, you may never try that business idea out.

This can happen with anything we want in life. A lot of these people are not evil, they are not bad, but that does not make them any less a thief, because what they continue to say to you is in opposition to what you want to do.

Some of their thieving ways may be subtle and some may be blatant, like saying that you can't do it or that you don't have the abilities to do it. How do they know you don't have the abilities needed? Are they saying it because they personally can't do it, so they put you in their place and say that you cannot do it? Straight-out thieves.

Don't ever let anyone steal your dreams, even if it is someone you love dearly. This person may think they are doing the right thing, but they are still a thief.

You must make sure that your security is the best that there is. Make sure that the trusted soldier standing guard at the entrance to the door of your mind is ever alert, never asleep, and constantly on guard against any words spoken to you which sound like the words of thieves. Make sure he does not let those words enter your mind. Keep your security at a high level so those thieving words never enter your subconscious mind.

Monitor your thoughts like good security guards monitor a priceless piece of art in a museum. Try and touch an ancient artefact in the Metropolitan Museum of Art in New York. If you do, you will soon hear a voice from the corner say, "No touching please." The guards are ever alert.

Stand guard and make sure your thoughts are positive.

Always positive? Yes, of course. Why would you want it any other way? Reject negative thinking and reject the words that thieves speak. Walk away from these thieves. If someone stands in front of you and tries to steal one of your dreams with negative words, walk away. Protect your thoughts like a mother bear would protect her little cub.

There is evil out there, to not realise that would be foolish. You may not come across it often but, if you do, fight evil with everything that you have. Protect your thoughts with all the strength that you have because the damage could be extensive if you don't. Your future happiness could be stolen from you forever, if you let it be stolen.

Find out where these thieves live and don't go there. Find out where these thieves work and don't work there. Find out where the thieves eat and eat somewhere else. Find the beach that these thieves lay on and vow never to set foot on the same sand. Don't go where they go and don't do what they do. They are thieves and there is no honour among these thieves.

If you find yourself confronted by the words of a thief, then reject them. If the words linger in your mind, replace the thieving thoughts with positive thoughts of what you want and the feelings that you will have when you get it. Reject the negative and replace it with the positive.

Visualise those dreams as if they have already come true and you are living them right now. Get lost in the visualisation. Let yourself smile when you think about it. Live it in your mind first, and then later you will live it in your life for real.

Recognise that the thief is just a thief, and you would not expect anything else from a thief. People may say that they would not try and steal your dreams, but that is not true, because they are thieves and thieves steal. We don't need to be surprised by this, we just need to know that this is the type of person we are encountering, and then simply continue on our way.

Know that you can live the successful life we have spoken about. It is your belief that has all the power. Even if the thief is lingering around you, your belief that you can succeed has much more power than their thieving words. Be the person now that you want to be in the future, act that way right now. I keep mentioning this because it works.

Let the thieves know that you have secured your mind, so they cannot break in and steal your dreams. They cannot steal your future away from you and your children.

It is what you do daily that makes all the difference in the world. There will always be thieves. Some will be far away from you and some will be close to you. The thief may not even know that they are a thief, but you will know. You will get that intuition and sirens will start to go off in your mind when you hear the words engraved on the hearts of thieves from the beginning of time.

When you are alerted, do something about it and walk away. Change your thinking and look to the future and just know that you are on your way, and that the thieves cannot influence you because they have no access to your mind. That is as secure as it will ever be, and you can be sure that you will have the life that you always wanted, if you let no one steal your dreams.

TWELVE

The great Florentine artist Michelangelo said that when he looked at a piece of marble, he could already see the statue inside the marble. All he had to do then was carve away what was not needed, and the statue would appear before his eyes.

Michelangelo was a creator. He created magnificent works of art in the Renaissance period. One of his greatest accomplishments was the statue of David, who defeated Goliath in the Bible story. He was commissioned to create a sculpture of this ancient figure, but he wanted the statue to reflect modern ideologies. Michelangelo wanted to create an idea, a purpose for the statue. At the time of its creation, Florence had exiled the powerful Medici family and they were now residing in Rome.

Florence was surrounded by many cities that threatened its survival. So, Michelangelo wanted to create this David as a symbol of Florence's strength, to show people that God was on the side of the Florentines.

He created the statue tall and, unlike other statues of David, there was no representation of Goliath or of David standing on his severed head. No, that was not the purpose of this statue, which was posed as if David was about to start heading in the direction of a battle soon to take place, with a facial expression to match. Michelangelo made David's right hand more pronounced than his left, symbolising God's strength. Even the direction the statue faced had meaning. The statue was looking straight towards Rome, where the exiled Medicis were living.

Michelangelo wanted this statue to show the people of the surrounding cities that Florence was ready for battle and that they were powerful. It was not your average sculpture.

Everyone creates in their life, either they create something good, or they create something bad. People don't know that with every thought they have they are creating something, whether it be good or bad. The key is to know exactly what you want to create. People may put much effort and much time into thinking about and planning for a two-week vacation, but then spend little or no time planning their day, their week, or even their life.

Create the life that you want to live. Don't just take whatever life throws your way. The life that you plan to create will be your reality and no one else's. You will find that people say that you need to be realistic in your life, but whose reality are they talking about? We all live on earth, but we live in different realities. A person who is poor lives in a different reality to a wealthy person. An unintelligent person lives in a different reality to an extremely intelligent person. A movie star lives in a different reality to the person who makes their coffee in the morning.

Albert Einstein said, "Reality is merely an illusion, albeit a persistent one."

Create your reality. Like I have mentioned many times already, the key is that you need to believe with all your heart that you can achieve the reality that you want. If you can do that, if you can first live that in your mind, then you will eventually live it for real in your life.

If your goal is to live life like only three percent of the population lives, then that is where your focus should go. If that is the case, then don't listen to the other ninety-seven percent and what they think you should do. You become what you think about. That is the source of creation.

We have great creative abilities inside of us, so first create your life in your mind. See it as already real, like a sculptor sees the finished artwork before he puts chisel to stone. When you build a house, you must already see it completed before you start laying the foundation. If someone comes along and asks what you are building, and you say that you don't know and that you are just laying bricks, they will escort you to a safe place. No, before you build a house, before you start, you have every little detail and measurement written down, so that you know exactly what you are building.

Now that you realise that you and you alone are the builder of your life, you need to have the specific details of what sort of life you want to build before you start building. Start seeing that life complete in your mind and then the universe will guide you to each step that you need to take to get you to that life.

You become what you think about. If you think like everyone else, then you become like everyone else. Think differently, think about what you want and act as if you already have it. What do you want your life to look like? Write it down. How much money do you want to make every month? Write it down. Do you want to be in a relationship? Do you want to travel? If so, where do you want to go? Write it down. Start sculpting, start creating the life that you want. Don't let chance and circumstance dictate what you will get. Decide what you want and understand that you alone can create it.

You can have, be, or do anything you want that you can believe in and that is in the realm of possibility for you. Knowing that, you can have almost anything in life, but start with the first step, don't jump to the end of the book and skip the pages in between, or the book won't make sense. Go from chapter to chapter and you will see the story unfold. That is the same with you. Know what you want and then take the next logical step, one after another, until you reach your goal while thinking and acting as if you're already there the whole time.

You become what you think about.

Reprogram your subconscious mind by continuing to think about what you want and feeling it, and in time you will override those limiting beliefs that you once had and you will realise that you can have, be, or do anything that you believe you can have, be, or do.

You have the creative abilities. You just need to do

a little reprogramming and cut out that negative mind virus that has plagued you for many years and never allow it to return.

Faith is what it is all about. Faith that you have amazing creative abilities. Faith that the universe is on your side and wants you to succeed. The universe is a partner with you along your journey as you continue to hold tight in your mind the life that you want. Then, just be an amazing actor. Each day put on an Oscar-winning performance by acting like the person that you want to become.

Your mind is a sacred temple. The only thing that can bring down this beautiful temple is a parade of one negative thought after another. As the ocean over time bombards rocks and cliffs, erosion will eventually eat away the cliff face. Don't let these negative thoughts similarly erode your path to universal success.

Look at your friends, at the people you spend time with, and if they are not going where you want to go, then give them some breathing room and limit how much time you spend with them. Have you ever finished a conversation with someone, either in person or over the phone, and not felt uplifted afterwards, but rather felt worse than before you started talking? If so, why were you having that conversation in the first place? Why would you converse with people regularly, where afterwards you did not feel better, more determined, and more inspired?

If you continue with these conversations, then you will become like these people you regularly communicate with. If you don't want to be like them or live the life that they are living, then limit that association. I am not saying don't ever talk to them, of course not. Just limit those conversations and expand conversations with people who inspire you, the people that you look up to, the people creating their lives to be the best that they can be and not just letting their lives be tossed about by the waves of life.

These people are hard to find but if you put in the effort at the start, you will find them and in time you will be drawn to them. You will be able to stand in a crowded party and somehow the universe will see to it that you meet such a successful person. The universe will arrange an introduction. That is universal attraction at its best.

Guard your mind. Guard it from the avalanche of bad news that is everywhere today. Turn the news off; you don't need to know about the horrors of the day.

Some may say that you will be living in a bubble and that you will be naïve about what is happening in the world. Yes, you will be living in a bubble, but you won't be naïve, because I am sure you are well aware of the horrors of the world, you are just choosing not to hear about these horrors every day when you wake up. Live in your bubble and bring others into it. Protect yourself as you go about creating your dream life.

Affirm to yourself what it is that you want. Don't just repeat affirmations over and over again without meaning or feeling. Get a small card and if you believe in a God or universal power, then write down that God is the source of your supply, that your needs are met in every moment of time. You give thanks for God's riches that are in your life because money comes to you easily and effortlessly.

In this sentence, your wealth and riches from God can be anything that you want, not necessarily monetary. If you don't believe in a Creator, then you can use the concept of infinite intelligence.

On the other side of the card, write the sentence, *I am so happy and grateful now that I have…* and finish the sentence in the positive.

Always carry this card in your pocket and pull it out and read it with feeling. This will put your mind in the creative mode and the right frequency for you to do, be, or have anything you want. These thoughts and feelings will keep you on the path towards what you want.

How many people will do this? My best guess is five percent. Don't be like the rest, take the action needed.

People love personal development books, but that's where they stop, they don't take the actions and steps necessary for them to create the life that they want to live. Be different and start following the suggestions mentioned in this book.

Michelangelo could have put that piece of marble in his workshop and just dreamt about what he would create. He could have sat back with a glass of wine in his hand, day in and day out, and just think about the David statue trapped in the marble. This is good, but if he wanted to make that David statue a reality and create it with powerful meaning, he needed to put chisel to marble. The hard part is not the chiselling part, not for an artist; the hard part is the picture of what the artist wants to create.

Get that picture in your mind and then start chiselling away at your life, at your attitudes, your personality, your goals, and every aspect of your life. Start chiselling away to create the beautiful life that you want to live and, if you do this, you will create a life which is a beautiful masterpiece.

THIRTEEN

In a world where every human seems to be labelled a slave of their surroundings, a world where people find it difficult to get from day to day. In a world where you look and see people crying out the word 'victim' to describe their life, amongst them dwells a different man.

The Free Man.

This individual can be either a man or a woman, young or old.

Look closely, because it is hard to determine who this man is.

He is not easily noticeable when you walk down the street.

He walks amongst us but blends in between us, so he is hard to find.

The Free Man wakes up every day and looks at life as a special gift, a gift that he is determined to cherish every day.

He doesn't complain about his day, he enjoys his day. He enjoys every minute of the day. He doesn't run away from difficult times, but looks at those times and discovers who he is because of those times.

The Free Man runs from no one or no thing. He is kind to everyone because he sees every individual as he sees himself, a gift, a special gift that cannot be bought or replaced.

The Free Man finds joy in the little things of life and when he walks down a street, he notices a little flower growing on its own and he reflects on the beauty of creation and is reassured of his own beauty.

The sun shines and the rain falls on the Free Man, like it does on all of us. When it does rain, the Free Man does not cover himself nor flee for cover. No, he walks in the rain. He is conscious of the sensation of water flowing over his body and takes pleasure as it trickles down his side. He is amazed because this water is a gift that sustains not only him, but all life on earth.

When the Free Man walks down the street and someone bumps into him, he doesn't get angry; he is glad that we are all living together and that we are not isolated.

He has no boundaries around him prohibiting entry, he has an open door for everyone who wants to enter his world and bring their unique gifts to share with him, just as he will share his with them.

When his fellow man gets glory for one thing or another, the Free Man is proud to see others standing in a place of happiness and joy. He does not compete for anything in life, because he not only loves himself but loves all humankind. He says, 'Why compete when we are all unique?'

The Free Man helps those who need help because

he realises that they may not have the strength to help themselves. He never condones unkindness but shuns unkind people because he realises that they enjoy inflicting pain and suffering on people and he has no time for such people.

The Free Man may be poor, he may be wealthy. He may be male or female. He may live in any land or in any culture. Look out for this man. You may spot him in your travels.

If you suspect someone to be a Free Man, listen to what he says and before not too long you may get an inkling that he is the one you have sought.

The Free Man is himself, whether at home or at a party, in a traffic jam, or stuck in an elevator. He does not let the happenings around him dictate how he will treat himself or treat others; of course not, he is free.

He doesn't need to pretend, because he just is.

You will never hear him complain or whine about anything because he loves every moment of existence despite life's circumstances.

The Free Man sees a child playing and he smiles at what he sees, pure innocence expressing itself in all its glory. An innocent child that has unending potential and unending imagination. He recognises the twinkle in the child's eye, which reminds him of the twinkle in his own eye.

When his culture says to do things a certain way, the Free Man weighs up if the culture's way is the best way for him, and if it is not then he refuses to comply.

He refuses to bow down to the terms of others, not in a rebellious manner but in a quiet manner, an assured manner, knowing that everyone must walk his own path and not the path of others.

The Free Man sees life as fun. He sees life as a comedy. Nothing can turn him away from joy and happiness. He accepts nature for what it is, a gift that has its own laws and runs its own show.

The Free Man does not live either in the future or in the past, but lives right now in the present, a time that he will never get back again.

He allows all his senses to take in each moment and is grateful and happy for these moments in his life.

The Free Man knows that the universe is on his side. Therefore, he knows that in the end things will work out for him if he has faith that they will.

He continues to live the best life he can live.

The Free Man only allows purity into his mind and turns away from anything that would defile his thinking. He knows that positive thinking all day, every day, is the source of all his power. Therefore, he protects his thoughts like a bank would protect its money.

The Free Man knows that there is poison around, but as long as he protects his thinking he will never notice this poison because the Free Man does not live in the same world as everyone else.

His world is created by his pure imagination and his imagination is what has created his world. He breathes the same air as we do, but does not experience the same things as everyone else does. He has hope, faith, and he believes. Therefore, he acts with those beliefs to strive every day to be the best human he can be. He strives for the best in kindness, thankfulness, gratefulness, and purity of soul.

He looks up at the stars and loves what he sees, endless beautiful expanding space.

The Free Man loves every expression of human creation, from works of art to songs of beauty, to the voices that put words to that beauty.

He appreciates these things because he knows they come from a higher source than the person performing these things for the world to see and hear.

The Free Man dreams of his life and then starts to create that life. There is nothing good or bad in the Free Man's world. It is only good or bad because of the meaning that he applies to each moment in his life.

He is not chained to life's challenges. No, he is a Free Man.

He has escaped the world that many today call their home and he vows never to return, he is free. He removed the shackles that held him back, and on that day he swore to himself that he would be free for all eternity.

The Free Man has no interest in changing the world because he did not create the world. The Free Man is interested in helping individuals in the world because he realises that, to be free, it must start with one man and then a second man, and in time more and more people will be free.

The Free Man wishes to wear no crown or expensive clothing. He does not wish to drive in the best vehicles or live in the most expensive homes.

No, the Free Man needs nothing external to validate the fact that he is free. He does not brag about his freedom. He does not draw undue attention to himself. He does not need attention to be free and, because of this, he will always remain free.

If the day comes where you spot the Free Man, go up to him and shake his hand and say 'thank you.' Thank you because you have encountered the Free Man and he is real and because of this encounter, and the knowledge that such a man exists, you now have the opportunity be like this man, free.

He is a man people have heard about for generations, stories have been told about the Free Man. Songs have been sung about him, but very few people know who he is. He walks amongst us looking for opportunities to help where help is required.

Can you or I spot the Free Man in a line-up? No, because his appearance is just like all of us.

The Free Man is here, he is there. Look out, because one day, you may encounter him, and you too can be free.

CONCLUSION

On Sunday 18th June 1815, Napoleon Bonaparte, a usually very competent leader, made a decision that led to his defeat. The night before the big battle at Waterloo in Belgium against a coalition of forces, the weather turned bad and it rained heavily, leaving the battleground wet and very soft. Because of the effect the soft ground would have on Napoleon's horses and the army's big guns, he waited until the afternoon to commence his attack.

This decision had a tragic result for the French forces because Napoleon assumed that the Prussian forces were far off, and that he could attack the coalition forces that afternoon before the Prussian reinforcements came. Unfortunately for the French, Napoleon was wrong about where the Prussian army was. By the afternoon, the Prussians had joined the coalition army and consequently Napoleon Bonaparte lost the battle at Waterloo.

Had he decided to attack in the morning before the Prussians arrived, Napoleon might have won the battle. Instead, his decision had ongoing tragic consequences for the French emperor.

Every day we decide. We make big decisions and we

make small decisions. Some decisions have few consequences and others have major consequences.

Now that you have arrived at the conclusion of this book, What will you do?

This was a question put to me many years ago while studying personal development. I had a decision to make; keep reading books and learning, just feeling good and going about my life, or take what I had learned and start to make a real effort to completely change my life?

I am so glad that I made the effort and started to apply what I had learned so I could change my life, and change my life I did. I don't even recognise the person I was a decade ago; that man is unknown to me. If I saw him in the mirror, I wouldn't know who he was.

I ask you that question again, What will you do now? Will you start making the right decisions and start to enact what you have learned so you can completely change your life? That is my wish for you to start today taking control of how you think, and once and for all saying to yourself that you will no longer be a passenger in your life. No, you will now and forever be the captain of your own ship, the captain of your life.

Guard your thoughts, protect them. Know that you are special. Of course you are, you are a human being with amazing abilities. Realise your abilities and value yourself, and do not tolerate anything or anyone that does not value you. Walk away from these people, don't entertain their ideas about you.

You can be, do, or have anything that you want. If you

take the steps outlined in this book and start applying them, you will start to see your life change. People will ask you, what are you doing differently to them?

You will be starting to create the life that you want, and I am sure that the thing that you want to create is a life of happiness and joy while you travel this journey through life.

Remember everything is energy, including you. We are all connected. Your thoughts have the power to create the life that you want. Turn away from focusing on what you don't want and start focusing on what you do want. You are the Michelangelo of your life.

This universe is full of abundance, and universal success will help you get what you want. Your purpose in life is what you, and no one else, say it is. Create that purpose, see to it that you are heading in that direction. Do things that bring you joy and happiness and eliminate things that make you unhappy, and you will soon find happiness waiting for you like an old friend.

Happiness will be the fuel of your success. Continue to put yourself in a happy, feel-good state and then focus on what you want and you will see this universe do remarkable things.

When you follow what makes you happy, you will live in a state of joy and you will be open to the abundance of the universe.

Follow your passion, follow what excites you, follow what will make you get out of bed early and back into bed late, because life is a magnificent gift and you should use that gift to the best of your abilities. You will do things that people say are impossible, but they won't be impossible for you.

You deserve to be happy, so leave all that you have been through in the past.

Negative things have no place in your future. Instead, look to the future with confidence and make sure that you are the creator of your destiny. Universal success is an art, so be the great artist of your life and create a magnificent masterpiece.

My wish for you is that you live a life of happiness, joy, success, and passion and that, on your journey through life, you enrich the lives of people around you. If you practise the art of universal success and start to change, then everything will change for you. That is my promise to you.

www.ingramcontent.com/pod-product-compliance
Lightning Source LLC
Chambersburg PA
CBHW021007090426
42738CB00007B/689